THE CLYACK SHEAF

To My Granddaughters
Linda, Donna, Gail and Julie

DAVID TOULMIN
Photograph by Jim Love. Courtesy of Aberdeen Journals Ltd.

THE
CLYACK SHEAF

(The last bound sheaf but not the end of the harvest)

Sketches of life and characters
in northeast Scotland

DAVID TOULMIN

ABERDEEN UNIVERSITY PRESS

First published 1986
Aberdeen University Press
A member of the Pergamon Group

The publisher acknowledges subsidy from the Scottish
Arts Council towards the publication of this volume.

British Library Cataloguing in Publication Data

Toulmin, David
    The clyack sheaf: sketches of life and
    characters in the North-East.
    Rn: John Reid   I. Title
    823'.914[F]   PR6070.078

    ISBN 0-08-034517-4

Printed in Great Britain
The Aberdeen University Press
Aberdeen

CONTENTS

ACKNOWLEDGEMENTS   ix

BREAD UPON THE WATERS   1

REAR-MIRROR LOOK AT THE PAST   6

SPRING OUTING   17

APPLE OF THE BOVINE WORLD   24

BOOTH OF DOWNIEHILLS   28

DOCTOR BRUCE OF INVERQUHOMERY   48

RAFAEL CARLOS GORDON   79

LAIRDS OF FOVERAN   87

PETER BUCHAN   94

ARTHUR GARDINER—GROCER POET OF DYCE   104

DEATH OF A FATHER   108

THE RELUCTANT RAT RACE   119

PLEASURABLY REMINDED   138

ACKNOWLEDGEMENTS

Acknowledgement and thanks are owing to several Buchan families for allowing me to interview, research and quote from their individual histories, genealogically and businesswise, in the composition of this book. Those I should like to mention are the MacIntosh family of Greystone farm, Peterhead; the Booth family of Downiehills, Peterhead; the Bruce family, late of Inverquhomery Estate, Longside; Peter Buchan, Doric poet, Peterhead; Mrs Gardiner and family of the late Arthur Gardiner, the grocer poet of Dyce, Aberdeen; and on Deeside Mr and Mrs James W Craig of the smiddy at Drumoak.

Thanks also are owing to Diane Morgan for permission to publish three of the articles which previously appeared in *Leopard Magazine*. These are 'Peter Buchan', 'The Lairds of Foveran' (*Leopard* title 'The Dragonfly of Foveran'), and 'Rafael Carlos Gordon' (former title 'The Spanish Connection'), in which Miss Morgan was associated in the genealogical research of the Gordons of Wardhouse, Beldorney and Kildrummy. All three pieces have been revised and rewritten since they first appeared in print. The version of 'Pleasurably Reminded' given here is quite different from the copy which appeared in *Leopard Magazine*.

I an indebted and offer my grateful thanks to Flora Garry for allowing me to quote from her father's (Archie Campbell's) obituary on James Booth of Downiehills, Peterhead, in the profile of 'Booth of Downiehills'.

David Toulmin
August 1986

BREAD UPON THE WATERS

My first memories of Buchan are of running behind the harvest carts loaded with sheaves and watching the two iron-rung wheels seemingly coming together below the axle. Of course they never came together but it was the sort of optical illusion which set a pattern for much of my outlook on life, in seeing things that others didn't seem to notice, or imagine I saw them, which was eventually to make me somewhat different from anyone else around me. Even before I was fourteen I regarded other loons and quines of my own age as children. I felt that I was the adult with grown-up ideas though I still didn't know the meaning of words like precocious and puberty. The Buchan schools taught me how to read and write but it was from the crofters I lived among that I got my education, from them and the farmers' wives who loaned me books, casting bread upon the waters in my hunger for knowledge.

Towards the end of my schooldays this fascination for cart wheels returned to me. I think it was because I realised the art involved in making them; not a factory made thing like the iron wheels on cars and motor lorries, but something that was done at the local joiner's shop, while the blacksmith next door fitted the wooden cart wheels with iron rims. They were massive things to me then, with naves (hubs) beautifully thirled in iron and the spokes and filleys (deep rims) in symetrical perfection, and when freshly painted and stencilled in different colours (as the lorry

1

wheels were) they were for me the ultimate in man's ingenuity.
Floats and gigs were likewise attired and I admired them all,
even the spanking gig wheels rimmed with solid rubber, as were
the motor vehicles of those days when the pneumatic tyre was just
beginning to appear.

I had even got the length of watching how long it took for a
film of rust to appear on the iron rings, and the crunch of metal
on stone grit roads was the music I listened to. If the farmer had
been to town with his float the rings were clear as a sixpence, but
in two days rust was forming, and by the end of a week they were
quite rusty, so I could tell by a glimpse in his cartshed when a
certain farmer had been away with his float (two-wheeled lorry)
which, besides the phaeton, gig or spring-cart was the farmer's
equivalent of the present day motor car.

I think I lost my interest in horse-cart wheels during my last
school holidays when I was thirteen. A local crofter called Josie
Dey asked me to go to the moss with him to wheel out peat in
barrows from the lairs for loading and carting home. There was
no mention of payment and the work was considered as just a way
of passing the time during my holidays. We took his late father's
old horse gig and with a flaggon of saps and a basket of scones
and 'lang ale' bottles filled with milk we set off for a day in the
peat-moss. Everything went well until we were half-way home in
the evening, spanking on in the gig when one of the iron tyres
came off and we were stottin' along on the spoke ends on the hard
bumpy road. We had to go back and collect the sections of wooden
filley (rim) we had lost on the road, and the iron hoop which had
careered into a ditch, and with lengths of wire stolen from a
farmer's fence we managed to bind up the wheel again. It took
us about an hour and I was famished, and we just managed to
limp home before the iron ring bit through the wire at the edges.

Josie then asked me for a turn at the hoe, the first time I had
ever 'hyowed' in my life, and he armed me with a short-handled
hoe 'to be nearer ma wark' and wedged me in the drills between
himself and his mother, so that they could keep an eye on my
work. And old Jeannie as they called her was sharp-eyed as a
ferret, and if I accidentally hoed out a turnip that should have
been left in the drill I got a gie kyardin', for she was sharp-
tongued as well. For a week's hyowin I got one shilling and an
old jacket that had become too small for Josie and all my food

except breakfast, which I had at home. My mother said it was an insult of course and that I shouldn't go near the place again.

About forty years later, after a long absence, I met Josie Dey again and reminded him on the gig episode but he could remember nothing of it, which says something for my own excellent memory, which has enabled me to write of these far off things that happened in my youth.

I also remember Josie's cow, referred to by the neighbours as 'the rims of Joy', I don't know why except that she was skin and bone, emaciated from tuberculosis, though Josie insisted it was ulcers, and his mother milked her three times a day until the old cow dropped dead and the knackery man came and took her away. Bovine tuberculosis was never discussed in those days, but looking back I am not surprised that Josie's father died of the disease. Josie fed his cow and two shelts on oats he crushed on the stone-flagged kitchen floor with a hammer in the winter evenings, because he couldn't afford a mechanical 'bruiser' or oat-crusher in his small barn, though he did have a threshing mill driven with horse-spars but never used it and hired portable threshing plant and sometimes forgot to pay the neighbours for their help.

One of the things that kept me going back to Josie's place was the beautifully bound three-volumed History of the Crimean War which had belonged to his father. Josie never looked at them, but from the day his mother first showed them to me, and not without a little pride in the possession of them, with their finely tooled binding and lavishly coloured illustrations, I gave her no peace until she allowed me longer time to study them. The tomes were kept in the ben-room and on no account would Old Jeannie allow me to take them home. After much 'priggin'', however, I was permitted to look at the books in the antiquely furnished 'best room' on a lace covered table by the light of a brass paraffin lamp and the blinds down, and on a winter's evening, while Josie hammered his oats on the kitchen floor I was pouring over the implications of Lord Raglan in the Charge of the Light Brigade, the nursing adventures of Florence Nightingale and the Siege of Sevastopol. This much I owed to Old Jeannie Dey. Nowhere else could I lay my hands on books like these, not even in the small school library, and nobody had ever told me there was a public library in the town. Those valued gilt-edged

Histories had been purchased by instalment payment by a hard working crofter who perhaps had more need of a healthier cow or new rings on his gig wheels, but that his enthusiasm for learning had overpowered his better scruples.

There were two other crofters that my mother visited in the winter evenings and I went along because they possessed those Histories of the World which had been bought at great expense and were harboured in the 'best room' out of sight of prying eyes who might have thought they were more in need of respectable armchairs or a new 'deace'. One of these crofters, old Sandy Bain, allowed me to take home two volumes at a time, *A History of the Great War*, which had finished about six years earlier, and I studied them closely and learned much from them on the futility of war. In another crofter's kitchen, while my mother gossiped with the family, I was engrossed with the triumph of the English King Edward III and the Black Prince over the French at the Battle of Crecy, and how the archers of Henry V had beaten them again at Agincourt, all of which was adding to my store of knowledge.

One of the crofters allowed me to play his horned gramophone, while another fixed me up with earphones and had me listed to his wireless crystal set. Much later in life, after I was married, an old shepherd loaned me all his *Chambers Encyclopedias*, which introduced me to European history and the lives of great men like Frederick the Great, Voltaire, Robespierre, Napoleon, Bismarck of Prussia and others, and I could browse over their biographies to my heart's content. That was how I became self-educated, not in the academies of learning but by the firesides of those obliging and kindly crofters with whom I associated in my boyhood. Not that mine was an all-embracing, comprehensive curriculum, but it served my needs.

I was disgraced however when old Roger Cassie roupit oot and coupit his rubbish on the heather. I rummaged the pile one fine Sunday afternoon and came upon an *Encyclopedia of General Knowledge* that stank with age and was soiled with tea-leaves and peat ash. It was rich in wood-cut illustrations, many of them biblical, and contained a survey on Haley's Comet, so I just had to have it, and giving it a good dicht with a tuft of girse and my hankie I got it under my oxter and carried it home. But mother wouldn't have it in the house; it had 'an aul' smell', she said, and sent me to the coalshed with it, where I resigned myself to its contents, reading at every opportunity, sitting on the coal with the door open for light. But it was a heavenly light and I was in the company of angels, the Patriarchy of the Old Testament, and they held aloft for me the Lamp of Learning and Wisdom, and I still remember my glorious find with the fondest of memories.

The bigger farmers paid me more than I got from Josie Dey. For a whole Saturday gatherin' tatties I got half-a-crown which gave me an evening at the pictures, a pie and chips supper, the Picture Show weekly, a Buffalo Bill novel and one of Sexton Blake, and counting tuppence for a Five o' Woodbines I still had eight pennies in old money left for another week's spending. It was more elastic in those days and stretched much further than our modern decimal coinage. I never went in much for sherbit bags or lucky tatties, Battle-axe treacola slabs, strippit ba's, readin' sweeties, Broch candy or lettered rock. A drag on the old man's pipe on the sly was worth more than all these grulshicks and better for my thought process by way of education.

REAR-MIRROR LOOK AT THE PAST

The other day I motored back some fifty-six years in time, over half-a-century to the very first farm I worked on in 1927. The farmer was waiting for me in the close, almost on the spot where his father engaged me as a loon to sort the nowt and work the orra-beast all those years ago. The old man died at eighty-three and his son is advancing in age, though still five years my junior, and his son Bill, grandson of my original boss, now runs the farm. Mr Willie MacIntosh of Greystone farm, in the Blackhills area of Peterhead, pointed out to me that we were within sight of the school (now closed) which we both attended and the farm of Springhill where my parents lived when I worked as a loon for his father, all within a two-mile area, where I was never out of sight of home, at the school or on his father's farm. 'Yet ye ran awa' twice in the first sax months', he reminded me and I had to admit to my truancy, several times at school and twice on the farm.

'And ye tel't the Pearl King ye ran awa' because ye didna like Bob Duncan, and the Pearl King tel't ye that ye wid get Bob Duncans far iver ye gaed.'

'Aye, and he was richt', I admitted. 'In later years I met a lot worse than Bob. Lookin' back Bob wasna a' that bad and maybe I needed a bit o' discipline. I think I lived tae reap the benefit o' Bob's strict rule and trainin', but a loon always thocht he was bein' ill-used on his first place.'

'Aye, Bob was a bit hard but he meant weel and he was weel liked. Peer stock, he didna live tae see retirement.'

'The first time I ran awa' ma mither took me back the next mornin' afore daylicht and chappit on the back kitchie door. Yer father got oot o's bed and cam' an' opened the door in his nicht-goon, and when he opened the door ma mither shoved me into the lobby beside him and said: 'That's him back!'

'Oh aye, woman', yer father said, 'But we wunna say nae mair aboot it; the laddie will get his brakfist and awa' back tae the nowt in the byre again.'

My mother did this because I hadn't completed my contract for the six months and I wasn't entitled to any wages until I did so. That wouldn't have been so bad but I ran home again before the Term and she had to take me back a second time, bribing me with Woodbines and reminding me how short a time it was until the Term when I could leave if I wanted to and I would get my full wages—£6. 10s. for the time I had worked. I wanted a job in the town but she wouldn't listen and neither would my father. The excuse this time was that I had a sore tooth and Mr MacIntosh never questioned me. He never looked in my mouthful of bright fresh ivories to see if an extraction had been necessary, but directed me back to the early morning byre work again. I think he suspected it was a ruse but he was a very lenient old gentleman.

My wages at the November Term cured me of my delinquency on the farms and I remained with Mr MacIntosh until my age and rising wages priced me out of his employment.

I began work at Greystone on a Saturday, the day after I left school on my fourteenth birthday, and it was for a whole day because there were no half-day holidays then. My first job was picking sprouts off the tatties in a sod pit behind the steading, on a site now occupied by a huge sprawling implement shed, where I would have been under a roof had it then existed. I had a clay pipe in my pocket and a little tobacco but I was afraid to light up until the farmer did so.

'Fut wye are ye nae smokin' yer pipe, laddie?' he enquired.

'Oh, I wis wytin or ee lichtit your een', I offered as explanation.

'Weel laddie, ye'll hae a lang time tae wyte 'cause I dinna smoke. But licht yer pipe man. I dinna mind ye haein' a smoke sae lang as ye hae a lid on yer pipe, an' it's less dangerous aboot the steadin' than smokin' fags.'

I'll never forget my first hay-cutting at Greystone. Bob Duncan that was foreman was on the mower with his pair of horses, Jimmy and Love on the drag-pole. There were two iron seats on the reaper, one on each side above the driving wheels, one for the driver and one for the man with the tilting-rake, who swathed the hay on to the cutting-bar—and that was poor me. Unfortunately, that first summer of my working life my legs were not long enough to reach the footrests and Bob was afraid I would loose my balance and fall in front of the cutting blade. Because of this deficiency he made me run behind the machine with the tilting-rake, which was enough for me to carry, never mind using it, and I was so tired out by nightfall that I couldn't sleep in my bed, for I was tilting hay half the night in a bewildering nightmare. By next summer I was big enough to get on the tilting seat and it almost made a man of me, which perhaps had been Bob's intention.

The hoeing season was another hardy start for me. Previously I had only hoed on Josie Dey's croft during school holidays, which was a soft job compared with hoeing in a squad, where I was supposed to keep up with the men. Because of this they made me hoe the ends of the drills, which was hardest of all where the horses had turned around with the implements and the ground was as hard as the road. This again was improved the second year when I was sandwiched between the foreman and the squad and had to make the best of it, but at least the ground was softer. This was the start of my forty-four seasons at the hoe, four to six weeks of every summer I worked on the farms, depending on the acreage, and I never missed one of them.

The worst thing that happened to me that first summer at Greystone was when a cow stood on the big-toe of my left foot while I chained her up for the milking. Thump as hard as I could she wouldn't budge and she stood there for at least three full minutes before I managed to dislodge her hard hoof from my injured foot. My big toe swelled until I couldn't get my boot off without a painful struggle and next morning I couldn't get it on again. Trying to keep up with Bob to the stable I had to hirple on one foot while dragging the other half inside my boot. It took half-an-hour of exercise and muscle warming exertion before I could get my stiffened toe sufficiently bent to enter my tackety boot, and even then it was murder for me to walk about, never mind working. This went on for weeks and months and Mrs MacIntosh took pity on me and gave me embrocation cream with which to massage the inflamed toe. Another relief was when she boiled a kettle of water and had me sit on a chair with my foot in a basin of hot water 'as het as ye can thole' to reduce the swelling. But all the time I had to keep up with Bob, limping at his heels like an injured dog. Eventually the nail came off and was replaced with a lump of horn like a ewe's hoof and I am left to this day with a hammer-toe, the joint still unyielding as the shaft of that instrument, while the horn toe has to be trimmed periodically with a garden secateurs.

The peats were another tussle, wheeling them out in a barrow from the soft lairs to the loading ramp in the Savoch Moss, where Mr MacIntosh worked a lair in the terms of his lease with the Merchant Maiden Company of Edinburgh, who were his lairds. My biggest worry was leading Love (Bob's mare) by the bridle on the rutted and bumpy cart track out of the moss to the main road, about a third of a mile distant. Bob went first with Jimmy, who was canny enough, but what with the rocking and swaying of the loaded carts and Love in a flurry and champing at the bit I was terrified she would put an iron hoof on the big toe of my other foot. I was always thankful when we reached the main road when Bob took both animals in hand and I could go back to my peat wheeling until he returned for the second trip of the day. I had my flaggon of bread-saps, oat-meal bread and cheese and some of old Amy's home-baked scones and rhubarb jam and milk to swill them down. I was almost alone in the peat-moss and the things that frightened me were weasels and lizards, because of the stories I had heard of folk being attacked by packs of weasels or bitten by a small snake we called an 'Esk'. I got a hurle home at eventide on top of Bob's second loaded cart, which took about an hour on the three-mile journey, the Jimmy horse out in front, glowering about him at all the crofts on the way: Whitebog, the Wright's croft, Jimmy Chalmer's place, Blackhills Kirk, the smiddy, Blackhills Home Farm, the Post-Office, Redleys, and when we came round the last bend with Greystone in sight Jimmy quickened his step and Love lagged a bit trying to keep up with him, his ears cocked forward in anticipation of his evening meal of crushed oats and having a roll on his back in the park with his heels in the air, his labours of the day forgotten.

The harvest of 1927 was the worst on record and in the midst of it our foreman Bob was removed to Aberdeen Royal Infirmary for an operation on the varicose veins in his legs. Consequently I had to learn to cut corn with a scythe, which was as heavy as the tilting-rake, and I was supposed to swing it like a sword in battle. While sharpening the blade with a short carborundum stone I sliced my right thumb down the middle and nearly bled to death before Old Amy, the farmer's sister managed to stop the flow.

However, I got over it all and was still on my feet when Bob returned to build the corn stacks about six weeks later. The harvest went on until the November Term that year and some were struggling with ruined crops into the New Year. The Harvest Thanksgiving was a bit of a joke and was blended in with the New Year celebrations, such as they were in those years of poverty.

It was a winter of terrific frost and the turnips were frozen to stone in the fields. There hadn't been time to store turnips in a clamp and the cattle couldn't eat them in the byre troughs. Mr MacIntosh had me bury two cart loads of swede turnips in the horse dung midden in the hope of thawing them. The horse midden was always kept separate from the cattle dung. It was considered more suitable as potato fertiliser and generated more heat and gave off more steam in the process of deterioration. Next day I wheeled warm pulpy turnips into the byres and the cattle sniffed at them and stood back from the troughs at the full length of their neck chains. Hunger however forced them to change their minds and eventually they dug their teeth into the turnips, thawing them still further with their warm breath. I got some of the swedes through the plump-hasher for the younger stirks with teething troubles but it was an uphill job, even with some assistance from the farmer, who had more weight than I had for the work.

I had just finished the evening feed when Lipton's van called at the farmhouse with the weekly groceries. There were two men with the van on the snow-blocked roads, and while the grocer delivered his provisions the driver, Tom Alexander by name, came over to the warm, lantern-lighted byre to straighten his legs

and get out of the cold. He knew absolutely nothing about farming and asked me if we fed the cattle on boiled turnips. I told him
that we did, and for once I wasn't really telling a lie, the blessing
was that while he stamped about to warm his feet it took his mind
off asking to see the boiler we used for the turnip menu. If he had
of course I would have taken him outside in the dark round the
corner of the steading to the horse midden. But of course he
wouldn't have believed me. In my forty-four years on the Buchen
farms I never again was asked to perform this function in bovine
cuisine.

By the time of my third spring at Greystone I was looking
down my nose at Bob; about half-a-head taller than he was
though not as broad and I had stopped running home to mother
with my tales of ill-treatment. I was even trusted with the three
horses in the three-tyned grubber while Bob planted the farm
garden. I had Jimmy and Love and my odd mare Rose (the orra-
beast) as a team and I was instructed to grub the hill park for
turnips above the steading and the mill-dam, a park that was
studded with submerged rock and gave the farm its name. Mr
MacIntosh even undertook to look after my cattle in the byres
so that I could get a few whole days on the job. His only instruction was that I 'keep oot anaeth the grubber han'le', which pro-
truded over my head from behind the cumbersome implement
and was liable to crash down on my head or shoulder when we
hit a fixed stone. 'But Jimmy kens far a' the steens are', he said,
trying to reassure me, 'and he'll slow doon when yer like tae hit
a steen, so ye wunna get hurtet. Jimmy likes tae stop onywye tae
get a look roon aboot tae see fut's goin' on. Faith man, that horse
is wiser than a lot o' the folk roon here aboot and if he could spick
he wid likely gie ye a' their fau'ts as weel!'

The grubber was a primitive smiddy-made version of the
modern spring-loaded cultivator and was replaced with the heavy
disc-harrows when the tractors took over. The three horses pulled
the grubber while you walked behind with the reins. The five-
tyned grubber was pulled by four horses and two men walked
behind, taking it in turn to pull down the handle at the rig ends.
When you reached the end of the rig you stopped the horses by
crying 'Whoa there!' and pulled down the handle to lever the
massive tynes or ploughshares out of the soil. This took all my
weight and I was sometimes off my feet on the soft earth swinging

on the handle to get it fixed in a ratchet on the frame of the three-wheeled implement. This done you turned your horse-team to go back in the opposite direction, stopped them again and disengaged the handle from the ratchet, so that the tynes slid into the earth again when the horses moved forward. The snag with this handle was that when one of the tynes struck a fast stone and was forced out of the ground on impact the handle came down with the pitch and force of a blacksmith's fore-hammer swung from the shoulder. It would have split your skull or shattered your shoulder blade with the horses at a brisk pace and that was what Mr MacIntosh was afraid of. But the horse team at Greystone, guided by Jimmy, the lead or 'land' horse was never at a brisk pace. From long years of experience Jimmy was instinctively aware of the location of every hidden stone on the farm, and when he heard or felt the grating of a tyne on a boulder he slowed down to let it slide over the obstruction, or to give you a chance to pull the handle down to assist this procedure, while the reins slackened in your hands. The two mares eased off or applied pressure on their yokes instinctively, according to Jimmy's movements, working perfectly as a team, even without the Horseman's Word, of which I knew absolutely nothing, and all of it was owing to Bob's excellent horsemanship and Jimmy's equestrian intelligence. From then on I respected Jimmy's judgement and easy-going pace and his sense in locating a stone fixture and he never let me down. I also noticed that he was, as Mr MacIntosh had said: 'An ull-fashioned kind o' a beast and liked to see a' the ferlies', and he really did take a good look round the countryside while he dallied over a stone. Furthermore he reminded me it was 'lowsin' (stopping) time' by refusing to leave the end of the rig nearest the farm. I didn't have a watch and couldn't argue, except that I was hungry, but sure enough when I looked around as Jimmy had done I observed Mr MacIntosh on the dam bank in front of the farmhouse waving us home. To watch Jimmy dip his bitted mouth in the cooling water of the cement trough after a day's work was a lesson in endurance and satisfaction and contentment worthy of human observation.

The harvest is late this year in the Blackhills area because of the wet spring. At the time of my visit to Greystone Mr MacIntosh hadn't begun, but because of our excellent summer he was confident of a good yield. From where we stood in

the farmyard, and while I gazed over the waving barley my
eyes alighted on the old ruined croft house in the furthest field.
I remembered the Sunday afternoon in late November, 1927,
when I was feeding the cattle, and happening to glance from
the byre door, I noticed one of the cottage chimneys smoking
profusely. Next time I came out both chimneys were smoking
heavily, and even while I gazed one window and then the other
turned red as a sunset and smoke was coming through the roof
tiles. I ran to the farmhouse and told Mr MacIntosh but as
there were few telephones in those days everything was
destroyed and a family rendered homeless by the time the
firemen arrived. My biggest regret was that the occupant of the
cottage, a Mr Wallace, had taken my bicycle for repairs in his
benroom, and next day after the blaze I saw the twisted frame
and buckled wheels lying in a corner under a deluge of roof
tiles. The family were not insured and Mrs Wallace had just
recently purchased a new drop-head Singer sewing-machine on
the instalment system and this too had been destroyed. She had
been trying to light the kitchen fire with paraffin and the flames
had spread so rapidly that they had managed to salvage very
little of their household belongings. Fortunately the three
children were unharmed and the parents survived in a haze of
shock and amazement that they could be burned out so quickly.
A charity dance was arranged and well attended in the school
hall at Blackhills to tide the family over their difficulties, but
henceforth I lost all trace of them. The ruin still survives in
Mr MacInthosh's field as a reminder to me of this calamity.
It was a ghost-like feature for several months after the event,
and had stopped me crossing the fields at night to my parents
home on the brae, and until the daylight lengthened in the
spring I walked round by the road.

It was in late august of 1930, while I was working at Greystone
that we had the most terrible thunderstorm in living memory. A
great many of my contemporaries still remember it and they all
agree that the likes of it has never happened again, possibly
because most of our electricity is bottled and tamed nowadays by
the Hydro-Electric System. I reminded Mr MacIntosh that we
were standing near the end-rig where his father and Bob and I
were tramp-coling the hay in stifling heat on the day that the sky
darkened before the storm. It began late on a Thursday evening

and raged until daylight next morning, when it subsided until noon on the Friday; then it came on again with even more frightening ferocity, with outbreaks of torrential rain and the sky as dark as nightfall.

During the night I had to get up with Bob to look at our horses in the field, to make sure they were not in a panic and tearing themselves on the barbed wire fences. There had been a terrific bang at midnight when we thought a chimney had been struck, and that was when Mr MacIntosh asked us to get up and look to the safety of the horses. I was completely terrified and held on to the tail of the foreman's coat with my eyes closed against the lightning flashes. But I still saw them under my closed lids, and when I opened my eyes occasionally the whole world was a blobbing wilderness of wild daylight, as if the sun were being switched on and off erratically like an electric bulb. Bob seemed to have no fear and he was my hero of the moment and I held on to him as if for dear life. It was like the shell-fire in the film of 'All Quiet on the Western Front' and the thunder was like the barking of the guns. We had to walk between two fences, one on each side of the farm road, and the lightning spun along the wires like liquid fire. We had no need of a lantern, because the sheet lightning opened up the countryside in a livid glare, revealing our horses a quarter of a mile away, grazing contentedly on the seemingly barren pasture, Jimmy and his two mares, and despite the conflagration he didn't even bother himself to raise his head and look around him. Seeing they were calm we didn't disturb them. Otherwise we would have taken them home to the shelter of the stables.

Next day was just as bad, the world dark at noon, forked lightning jabbing out of the sky and the thunder almost one continuous bombardment. We sat most of the afternoon in the farm kitchen, I with my head in my hands in a corner, away from the window and the lightning flashes, while the dog growled incessantly from under the table. Old Amy sat behind the door, the lightning glinting on her gold-rimmed spectacles, while she occasionally muttered to the foreman: 'Isn't 'at affa' Bob!' But Bob sat calmly at the head of the table, his black-lashed eyes bright and fearless in the gloomy kitchen, while the smoke from his fag curled to the roof beams.

About four in the afternoon the storm eased somewhat and the

rain became heavier. Bob put on his overcoat and went to escort
the farm bairns home from the school, the present Mr MacIntosh
Senior and his two sisters Annie and Mary, alas now dead, and
he said he still remembered how glad they were to see Bob
Duncan that day, when the dominie, Mr George Reid, had kept
all the bairns in school until the end of the storm.

At the height of this storm in 1930 Princess Margaret was born
at Glamis Castle in Forfarshire. This we learned later, and also
that several animals had been killed in the fields, cows, horses and
sheep, and a farm worker at Crimond who had been working at
a fence. Farmers who had animals killed by lightning later
reported that the bodies never stiffened. Our chimneys had not
been hit and are still intact today.

Greystone farm steading has been altered and extended to
some extent and young Bill MacIntosh, grandson of my old boss,
who now supervises the working of the place told me I was just
in time to see my old byres exactly as I left them half-a-century
ago, even to the wooden straw hakes suspended from the stone
walls and the travis posts still in position. Within a short space
of time these also will be discarded and the walls altered to suit
modern requirements in animal husbandry. The present Mr
MacIntosh senior bought his farm from the Merchant Maiden
Company of Edinburgh so he is now his own laird and can proceed unhindered with future planning. The mill-dam has been
filled in and the water-wheel has gone but the old threshing mill
was still in the barn to remind me of my youth.

Meantime I had the privilege of standing in the byres where
I fed the cattle all those long years ago, where I worked and
dreamed my dreams and was now in a position of having seen
most of them come true and my mission in life almost fulfilled.
There are not many who are blessed with this sort of satisfaction
and I am indeed an honoured guest of Fortune to have survived
and witnessed such achievement of purpose. I knew not then
whither I was going but I have arrived safely from nowhere and
I am grateful to have been on this journey through life and time.

Young Bill has built an ultra modern wood and glass sun porch
in front of the old kitchen door, behind which was the sink where
his mother washed the dishes and we washed and shaved, but this
has been removed and I turned right into the old kitchen which
has also been modernised. The old peat-burning fireplace and

gantry have been supplanted by an up-to-date counterpart and the old wood linings have been stripped from the walls, now papered in contemporary style. The stone slabs have been lifted from the floor and replaced with wall-to-wall carpeting. Because there was no kitchenmaid I had on several occasions scrubbed and washed these slabs, and when the vanman called Old Amy had me hide myself under the kitchen table in case he came inside with the groceries.

The highlight of my visit was when the present Mrs MacIntosh took me through to the Green Room with the shuttered window where I ran my film shows for the family and neighbours, a somewhat dangerous enterprise in the days before electric light when I beamed a gas jet through glass on highly inflammable celluloid.

'Ye charged sixpence a time tae visitors, I mind that!' Mr MacIntosh concluded. And I excused myself with the cost of hiring films and the high price of acetylene gas. But they were wonderful days I spent at Greystone and I shall never forget them.

Mrs MacIntosh took me further along the passage to Old Amy's room (her husband's spinster aunt *who was* long since dead) and for me it was like a scene from David Copperfield while I gazed through the curtained windows at the sunlit garden, and when two of her grandchildren appeared at the door the picture was complete. I felt like Charles Dickens on holiday visiting a shrine of my long vanished youth.

Greystone farm was reflected in my rear-mirror as I drove away, receding into the past again with my youth and its memories, while I headed cheerfully into old-age and oblivion.

The Jimmy horse ended his working life in blindness and was retired for four years when he had to be put down because he couldn't get on his feet. This was in 1938 and was one of the last farrier cases attended by the kenspeckle Johnnie Beattie, the renowned Longside veterinary surgeon who practised for many years in the district. 'The horsie's like masell', he remarked, 'jist an aul' mannie gyan deen!' I always associate Beattie with the G S Morris version of 'The Buchan Vet', and he could have been the authentic original of this rollicking ballad.

SPRING OUTING

We had been housebound all winter, and in early April, tired of looking at the fower waas we did a bit of spring cleaning and then set off for a run in the car. It was a glorious day and the sun was busy with his paint brush from a palette sky of hazeless blue, garnishing the countryside with the colours of the season, mostly black, dull brown and green where cultivation was in progress.

We called at our son's home at Westhill because Jack is a bit of a mechanic and there was a girn in the front wheel of our Viva at the driver's side. He jacked up the car and spun the wheel and a tiny pebble fell out of the brake drum, so he didn't think that the bearing had gone. The wheel spun smoothly and was tight enough so he lowered the jack and we set off again on the road.

We had tea by the roadside in the woods above Cullerlie and everything went well until we left Banchory on the way home when the girn began again. By the time I reached Crathes the noise was like a metal grinder in a scrapyard. I stopped to have a look but the hub-cap was still cold so I decided to carry on in third gear until I reached a phone or a garage, which ever came first, and it was the smiddy at Drumoak.

I knew about Jim Craig and his show-piece traction-engine and there was just the chance that he could assist me. But Jim had retired and his wife said he was 'roon the back hackin' sticks', but if I cared I could use her phone. She is such a lively person, outgoing and friendly that while we waited for Jack to come to our assistance we were like old acquaintances, and she got my wife out of the car to show her the flower beds that decorate the front of the smiddy house. 'Oh I dee a' the gair-denin',' she laughed, 'and I polish the traction-engine forbye!'

When Mr Craig appeared I jokingly implied that I had come for his traction road-roller, which I knew was stationed some-where on the premises. 'Och bit 'ats a' richt,' he smiled, 'sae lang as ye leave plenty siller for 'er ye can tak' it!' But of course I knew that even if I could afford it (which I couldn't) the old blacksmith would never part with his steam-engine, 'Eileen' as he has christened her, after his daughter.

'Maist likely ye've run a bearin,' he suggested, 'We hid anither lad here the ither day wi' the same complaint, bit man, his wheel wis reid het—ye're nae sae bad's 'at.'

Our son Jack arrived with his Volkswagen van and diagnosed a smashed bearing, which meant we would have to leave the car at the smiddy overnight until a replacement could be procured in Aberdeen. Mr Craig instructed me to park the car behind the smiddy out of sight. 'Gin ye leave 'er at the roadside the loons micht hae the wheels aff o' 'er or mornin'!' And we keckled and leuch at the suggestion.

Jack propped up the car and took the wheel off and removed the hub casing and put it in his van and we drove back with him to Westhill for supper. His wife Lorna drove us back to the city in the evening so that Jack could go to bed because he is on a night-shift job. He goes to bed in the morning again but would be up by one o'clock in the afternoon and would drive us back to Drumoak. Lorna would get a new bearing in the forenoon and take us back to Westhill just after noon when Jack would be rising.

Next day, when Jack drove us back to the smiddy, and while he worked at the car, his mother and I had a longer crack with the Craigs, both man and wife, greatly to our profit and enjoy-ment, for they are of our own age-group and background and we had much to share and talk about.

It was another lovely day and my wife spent her time with Mrs Craig in garden and house, sharing the family matters that kindred women talk about, knitting included, which my wife cannot perform nowadays because of her painful arthritis. While our son worked at the car James W Craig unfolded his life story to me while he leaned against 'Eileen' under a tarpaulin sheet in a big shed behind the smiddy. The roof of the shed had fallen in and was leaning on the engine canopy and on the cab of a vintage Scammel unit belonging to Jim Craig junior for transporting the engine to the summer shows. 'The reef fell in this winter wi' a' yon wecht o' sna'. I niver saw the like o' yon afore!'

Apart from my moustache he is almost my twin brother for build and looks, and just as bald as I am when he removes his cap. The full moon in a queer place ye micht say. 'I'm a year aul'er than you though', he remarked. 'I left school at fourteen in 1926 when my father was cottared at Balquhindachy o' Methlick. He was heid bailie (cattleman) there and he took a day aff and took me tae the feein' market at Maud. He fee-ed me tae a placie at Auld Whaat o' New Deer and I got nine powin for the sax month.

'Fegs but it wis hard wark bein' a loon in those days. The next placie I gaed till I took on the third pair, but man I wasna fit for't and I ran awa'. I wis jist a bit halflin ye see and I couldna keep up wi' the foreman and the second lad fillin' muck. We wis muckin' in the dreels for neeps on a steep brae and I jist couldna keep my balance on the cairt. I nearly fell oot owre twa three times and back in the midden the foreman wis hame wi' his teem cairt or I hid a graipfu' or twa in o' my ane. Oh they were fit strappin' chiels and they could fair stammack their brose and wark gaed them nae bother at a'. I got a lad that I ken't tae gie me a cairry wi' ma kist tae the end o' the fairm road for the cairrier and sent it hame.

'Fin I appeared at hame ae day at denner time ma mither spiert fut I wis deein' here at this time o' day? I said I hid run awa' fae ma place. "Weel", she said, "Ye'll get nae bed here till ye ging back!" My grandfadder wis bidin' we's at the time and he said the fairmer wid get me in the jile for rinnin' awa'. I said I wisna carin' fut he did I wisna gaun back onywye. Ah weel, I got a bite o' denner and they didna throw me oot but it wis sair against their grain that a loon o' theirs couldna bide at his place. I got some o' the siller I'd vrocht for wi' a bit o' a thraw!

'Some places wis affa bare maitet. There wis ae fairm I wis at faur wi got a wee jarie o' treacle the piece tae last a hale week and the fairmer's wife keepit it on the warm range tae mak' it thin so that it spread farer on yer loaf. Mine wis a' deen or the middle o' the week and I hid tae chaw dry loaf efter 'at. The only time ye got a decent supper wis on a Sunday nicht fin ye wis toon-keeper and jist yersel', and that wis only eence a month.

'I feenished up as third horseman at Bogfechel o' Newmachar and then I gaed tae John Holmes in Inverurie tae start the smithin'. Fower shullins a wick I got and my mait, but nae at wick-eynes, I hid tae ging hame for that and of coorse as trades-men we got the half-day on Setterday. But the smiddy wark wis nearly jist as bad: sheein' clickit horse wis the very devil's wark and sometimes ye couldna get near them for kickin'; chep they waar, aboot a fiver the piece, niver been broken in, niver been handled and the wudmen bocht them for haulin' oot trees, but they had tae be shod—in those days onywye. And there wis nae set hoors in the smiddy; nae denner hoor if there wis horse wytin tae be shod, jist swally yer denner and back tae the anvil again. And some o' the smiths were as crabbit as the fairmers and they a' likeit a gweed tear o' wark.'

Our Jack had finished with the car by now and joined in our conversation, and being himself a vintage enthusiast he had plenty to chat about with Mr Craig. We got the pedigree of the Fowler engine from the day in 1966 he bought it for £150 from a scrap merchant in Peterhead. Now the 12 ton relic would fetch something like £20,000 from the connoisseur market.

'But she wis a randy fin we bocht 'er and ran awa' on the road. The throttle aye got stuck and ye couldna reduce speed or stop; tug as ye micht on the lever there wis nae response and it wis dangerous. It took months tae sort that an a lot o' patience.'

He drew the shape of the steam box for us on a piece of wood and explained the steam jet aperture that had worn beyond its normal size and couldn't control the speed. 'And then we scraped an inch of tar off her belly from working on the roads. Every nut and bolt we examined and repaired and we hiv a certificate for the biler. She'll need a bit polish but she's ready for the road again. We hinna been at the shows for twa 'ear but we're gaun oot this simmer again.

'Come awa' and hae a look at some o' the horse implements in the parkie here. See that langboord sock ploo there—efter a day ahin that thing ye wis fairly able for yer brose, thick as ye could steer them, a gweed bowlfu' that wid stick tae yer ribs and keep ye gaun for anither day's wark.'

I pointed to an Oliver plough with wooden stilts, a favourite in the old days with the horsemen and reputedly light and easy to handle. But not so easy on the horses according to Mr Craig: 'Look at the depth o' that boord (indicating the ploughshare or body of the plough). She took a great depth o' a furr though she wis swuppert and easy tae furl roon on the endrig eence she wis oot o' the grun. Oliver wis an Ayrshire man as far as I ken. He gid awa' till America and startet makin' tracters and they were sent across here the time o' the war.'

Other exhibits included a horse mill-course spar and pinions that could be adapted for threshing, corn-crushing, kibbling or breaking oil-cake for cattle feed. A one-horse Massey-Harris reaper stood in a corner of the field while under a roof was a small threshing mill with grooved roller feeding system and a spiked wooden drum for straw delivery. Mr Craig, with eyes beaming declared: 'I bocht it for a fiver fae an' aul' crafter wifie up in Strathdon, awa' at the back o' beyond. Ye can caa't bi han' if ye like. The folk up there ie threesh on a Sunday so that they could get a help fae folk in aboot for the day.'

He showed us another hand-driven threshing mill 'in a sheddie roon the back', no bigger than a barn-fan, the smallest specimen I have ever seen. I was standing on the concrete slab covering the old well near the hand-pump that used to supply water for the smiddy folk and the joiner next door—now discontinued. 'That waal's as deep ye can hardly see the watter at the boddom o't. Bonnie biggit, richt fae the foon. The vricht ees't tae cairry his watter in zinc pails on a frame kis he hid farrer tae ging than we hid.' I surmised that it had been very convenient having the joiner next door to the smiddy, especially for the ringing of cart wheels. 'Oh aye, he made the cairt wheels and roud them roon here and I put iron rings on them, het fae the fire we kennelt in the close, and mountin's on the naves (hubs) forbye. But that's a' feenished noo wi' the rubber tyres.'

We were then escorted into his small office at the mou' o' the close, where the Royal Coat of Arms is proudly displayed on the back wall facing the door: 'By Appointment to Her Majesty the Queen', for the wrought ironwork he had executed at Balmoral and on the Birkhall estates for the Queen Mother. 'It eence tae be abeen the smiddy door,' he mused, 'bit I hid tae tak' it doon fin I retired.' He is now seventy-one but looks fifty-five and his wife is equally resilient, with the smile of youth still on her lips and shining in her eyes.

A cabinet display of the many prizes he has won at the vintage rallies with the traction-roller stands in a corner. Pictures of horses and engines adorn the walls and he pulled out a drawer from another cabinet laden with harness decoration; not the modern plastic imitation but real leather and nickel plate rosettes and martingales that the enthusiasts are clamouring for. His desk drawers are crammed with mechanic magazines and showyard paraphernalia, and while he was exhibiting these Mrs Craig and my wife came to the door. 'A' that orra-dirt,' she joked, 'if I could get 'im awa' fae hame for a day or twa I wid hae a richt redd-up in there. The trouble is he niver gyangs fae hame, wunna leave the place, an' I'm feart tae tak' the car and ging masel' kis I micht hae tae polish it fin I come hame. He's that fussy ye see!'

But the smith was not to be outdone. 'Och bit she's jist as bad,' he grinned, 'that's the wye we hiv sic a little hoose, kis fin I gyang fae hame there's ie anither faul o' paper gings on the waa's!'

It is a very substantial old building and certainly not small but this was just his way of putting it in the banter with his wife.

Across in the smiddy something had gone wrong with the electricity and the cooker in the kitchen wouldn't heat. 'I'm nae carin' for the licht,' said her man. 'It's something tae mak' the supper I'm worried aboot!' But before he spoke another word his wife was rinkin on top of a smiddy implement and had the power switched off and the lid of the box opened while she examined the fuses. 'Oh she mends a' the fuses,' her man confessed. 'I'm nae an electrician and I wadna touch the stuff.' It turned out to be something wrong with the wiring outside and they had to 'phone Banchory for a sparkie. 'Ye'll jist hae tae gyang tae Bunchrie for a fish supper the nicht aul' man,' she suggested.

When the women had gone outside Mr Craig gave Jack and myself some of the history of the smiddy and the blacksmiths he had worked with before he came to Drumoak thirty-seven years ago. 'I used tae hae five men here and niver less than three, my ain son included for thirteen year, but fin the ile-boom startet they a' left ane by ane for bigger money and I was left masel'. They sleepit in the bothy there up in the rafters.'

Of the old blacksmiths—'Aul so-and-so wis the warst, a tirrin for wark and grand at the sheein' but a fule brute forbye. He

chawed tibacca and spat a' owre the place and pished amo' the
coal, and ye could hardly work aside 'im at the het forge in a
mornin' for the stink!'

But now it was time for us to go. We had enjoyed such a
hilarious afternoon that we had forgotten about the breakdown
that had brought us here in the first place. Jack reminded his
mother to get her 'moobag' out of his van and Mrs Craig took
a fit of laughing. She had never heard of a lady's handbag being
referred to as a horse's 'mou'-bag'. But this is our Jack's brand
of humour and it fair kittled her up. Everybody seemed to have
enjoyed our chance meeting and the worn ball-race seemed a
blessing in disguise. A body niver kens fut a day may bring forth
as they say.

When Jack had gone with his van I got into our car and said
farewell. 'We'll hae hinnert ye the day,' my wife remarked. 'Na
na,' said James Craig, bending down to speak to us, 'naebudy
hinners me nooadays. I've a' the time in the warld tae spick tae
folk!'

'We like tae be hinnert', his wife added, from which we de-
duced that they had enjoyed our company.

I started the car and moved on to the North Deeside road in
the direction of Aberdeen. 'Mind on yer moobag!' came after me
and I knew that Mrs Craig would be laughing.

But the girn had gone from our front wheel and we spun
quietly on the road for home. 'I think we'll hae a fish-supper in
a the nicht', my wife suggested.

'That's a grand idea,' I mumbled.

APPLE OF THE BOVINE WORLD

'Let the infernal rumble never cease!' Thus cried a certain Buchan farmer to his chaumer chiels in the old days of the horses, while his men thundered the swedish turnips into the wooden carts, ensuring that they hardly got their backs straightened for nearly ten hours a day, driving home the neeps for the nowt in the byres.

And it was just as hard for the bailies or stockmen topping and tailing turnips they plucked from the drills between byre times, bending over the long rows of glistening swedes, like cannon balls on an assembly line, waiting to be thrown into the gun-breach, and when the horse carts arrived the bombardment would commence.

But the 'infernal rumble' did cease, and was for a time almost completely silenced with the coming of the tractors and mechanical silage making, the modern substitute to the slavery of turnip harvesting. Rising wages and labour shortage almost finished the turnip as the staple diet for cattle, the apple of the bovine world, and grass ensilage became the universal provender.

But over the years silage has become just as expensive to handle as the traditional turnip, and the problems of cropping and silage effluent even moreso, while precision sowing and dressing of turnip seed with a suitable insecticide, and pre-spraying with weed-killers to minimise hoeing, together with mechanised harvesting has brought the much despised turnip back into favour. Farmers seem to be winning the battle against weeds thrashed out on the stubble by the combine-harvesters and turnip crops are clean again. Scattered on the fields for cattle feeding or netted for sheep in the spring the turnip has found a new venue from the old method of hand-feeding in byres. The turnip acreage is rising yearly, though with silage as an alternative stand-by it may never reach the proportions of the old days of cheap hand labour.

Almost any of the older generation of farmers will agree there is nothing to equal good swedish turnips and hay to produce beef or milk. The younger farmers may not agree, because they haven't really tried it, whereas their fathers had a foot in both worlds.

The turnip *brassica napus* is described as an annual cruciferous plant grown for its thick fleshy root or bulb. But it has a lot more to its credit than that. What other vegetable can survive with it in our bitter North-East semi-arctic climate?—standing naked and exposed in the drills all winter, while other root crops are insulated in sheds or earth clamps. Some varieties are almost entirely frost resistant (except in the harshest conditions) and once established in the drills weeds cannot smother them.

The turnip is rich in nutrient qualities, and in tons per acre it will rival anything except perhaps the potato, expanding in growth propensity from a small tablespoonful of seed to a bumper waggon load of rich juicy swedes.

The 'neep' came to Scotland nearly a century after it had become a field crop in England; and even almost as important to us, or even moreso (and certainly more profitable) than the Union of the Parliaments in 1707. Scottish MPs were impressed by the thriving fields of English turnips on their journeys to London by stage-coach in the eighteenth century.

In the previous century turnips were grown as a garden vegetable by Barclay of Ury House, near Stonehaven. In 1672 the Baron's Court dealt with a complaint by the Laird's gardener that the dykes surrounding the orchard were being broken down and 'Turnepes' stolen. The spelling here gives us a clue to the Doric expression of the word 'neep' for turnip, perhaps originating from the olde English 'naep'. In Ayrshire it became the 'Tumshie' and 'Turmit' in parts of England, but most Scotsmen still know it as the 'neep'. 'Neeps man, neeps', as we used to say, 'as big as yer heid!'

Robert Scott of Dunninald, tenant of Milton of Mathers, in St Cyrus Parish, was Scotland's pioneer of the new vegetable in 1754. Ten years later, William Lyall, at Wattieston, Fourdon, raised an acre and sold them at a penny a stone for kitchen use, a curiosity at the time, and crowds of people assembled to sample the new plant. Nowadays I pay 60p for a neep!

A later Barclay of Ury grew 130 acres in a season, an experiment which resulted in the growing of turnips for winter feed and the fattening of cattle and for the production of milk. The process expanded over the years and embraced the whole of the British Isles, revolutionising the structure of farm buildings, byres and steadings to hold more cattle, providing more milk for the nation and meat for everyone who could afford it.

The cattle population increased enormously, producing more dung and improving land fertility. 'The Carrying Days' were over, when farmers and crofters had to carry or support their half-starved cattle from the byres to the grass fields in springtime, having been kept alive all winter by eating chopped whins and straw. Now they lept out at the byre doors in rodeo fashion, tails in the air, in maniac, blissful freedom, and tore across the fields.

From being vegetarians people became meat eaters more than ever before. The production and distribution of meat became big business, with new butcher shops and abattoirs opening up all over the country, and the farmers responded by adopting crop rotation and fencing and dykeing their fields.

Artificial fertilisers, mixed with bone-meal (ground bones from the slaughterhouses) came in the 1830s, when phosphates were discovered as best suited for turnip growing. The manure distributor followed and came to be known as the 'bone-davie', most likely from its use in scattering the bone-meal and slag on the turnip fields.

Linseed oil and cotton by-products were processed into cattle cake for consumption with turnips and hay in winter; besides draff from the distilleries, mixed with crushed oats, bran or locust beans to obtain a balanced ration, with molassine treacle as a gentle laxative. Turnips provided the moisture where water was not always available, especially with cattle chained in byres.

But of course there were complications, and with the increased bovine population they were more prone to disease. Renderpest was rife and animals infected with the disease were isolated in stone buildings. Then there were the Foot and Mouth epidemics and a great many animals had to be slaughtered. Anthrax was deadly and infected humans, carried by the hair used in shaving brush manufacture. The disease was spread on the fields with the ground bones from infected animals. Eventually infected carcasses were burned or buried in lime and shaving brushes were sold 'Guaranteed Free From Anthrax'. Shoe leather was also suspect but perhaps in butcher products cooking eliminated some of the risks. Penicillin has subdued the terminal effects of anthrax but in the worst cattle plagues prevention rather than cure has been the norm in veterinary practice.

There are several claimants for the invention of the 'Bobbin-John', an instrument for the sowing of turnips by hand, before the turnip or 'neep-seed barra' became popular. Down in the Mearns they claim that Barclay of Ury was first with this instrument while we in Buchan give credit for the invention to the Laird of Udny.

In 1856 the Scottish turnip acreage was 460,000; in 1879 it was 491,000, a peak period, for by 1953, in competition with silage the figure had dropped by nearly half to 278,000 acres, and by 1964 it was reduced to 197,000 acres. From 7,000,000 tons in 1900 the weight of Scotland's turnip crop dropped to 5,000,000 by 1954. In the 1960s the nation's turnip crop reached an all time low, some farmers reducing their acreage by three-quarters, from forty acres to ten, while adopting the new forage-harvesters for grass ensilage.

The 'Turnepe' as a field crop was first suggested by an English writer in the sixteenth century, and Hallowe'en popularised it with the kids as a mask or candle-lantern.

The neep may never recapture its popularity in competition with silage, whether grass beans or tares, but at least it has been proved that silage (in tower or clamp) hasn't finished the turnip and there may be room for both in progressive economic farming.

The 'infernal rumble' may never be heard again for the noise of machinery, but the turnip will be on the assembly-line basis in factory farm progress.

BOOTH OF DOWNIEHILLS

I was on my way from Aberdeen to interview Mr Ewan Booth of Downiehills farm, near Peterhead (full name James Ewan Booth) when I met one of his articulated refrigerator vans at Balmedie, loaded with chilled meat for one of the English distribution centres. It was a beautiful August morning and huge golden toilet rolls of straw littered the stubble fields of harvest, a nostalgic reflection on my days of the stooks, and fields were being ploughed for next year's crop, a farming programme that seems light years away from my youth. When I reached Downiehills two more huge white vans were standing in the yard, with EWAN BOOTH, Fridge Freight Distribution painted in large blue letters on the sides. Mr Booth owns twelve of these vans and they collect Buchan meat from the abattoirs at Turriff and Portlethen for the English markets. The second dock strike of the 1984 summer had just begun, but as the Booth vans don't go to Europe (except with a special consignment) the strike didn't effect them much.

Now I spent the first half of my life in the Buchan Howes, a period of thirty-six years, yet I had never been to Downiehills. Na na, that wis faur Bailie Booth bade, and unless ye kent some o' the folk that were cottared there, and mabee had a quine that ye fancied, ye didna venture in aboot; nae unless ye wis lookin' for a fee, and 'cause his folk bade sic a lang time in his service there wis little chance o' that. Now in my seventies and retired,

28

and elevated from a bicycle to a motor car, I swung boldly into
the long beech-hedged avenue and made my approach to the big
hoose with its lodge-eaved roofs and handsome chimneys showing above the trees from the Longside-Peterhead road.

I drove in under the giant whale-bone jaws which form a
Gothic arch at the east side-entrance and felt at once like poor
Jonah in the Leviathan's belly. Mr Booth drives fish as often as
meat and for the marine side of the business those 'Jaws' are an
appropriate trade-mark, and they have stood there since his
grandfather built the mansion house in 1898. Before they were
blown down in 1983 from ground erosion they would have been
just tall enough to admit a refrigerator van; this time the roots
have been cemented into stone pedestals for another hundred
years' duration.

Mrs Joan Booth later breathed life into the dried bone structure by showing me the channels for the arteries and blood
vessels, where you could drop a pea into eternal oblivion; but at
the same time with her charming manner and ready smile she
rescued me completely from the apprehension of the whale's
belly. She told me that she was a Garioch quine and that she had
never seen Bailie Booth; that he had died the year before she
married Ewan. Her maiden name had been Joan Gray and her
parents had farmed Pitinan, near Oldmeldrum.

Entering the gracious late Victorian mansion from the back
kitchen door I was conducted by a maid to the hall, where I met
Mr Booth, a sun-scorched rugged six-footer in jersey and casuals,
keen-eyed and friendly, who immediately dispensed with for-
malities and escorted me to the office and computer room, the
heart, pulse and nerve-centre of the refrigeration distribution
service, where all the buttons are pressed and the figures tabu-
lated. Here I was introduced to the manager, Mr David May,
and secretary Mrs Catriona Baxter, and both looked up from
their work and shook hands with me. 'Of coorse my grandfather
niver saw a computer,' quipped Mr Booth. 'Nae likely,' I
replied, 'the only thing they filled in in those days was the Record
of Movement of Stock Book, and that was compulsory, itherwise
the fairmer's wife did most o' the clerkin'.'

Mrs. Booth brought us coffee in the west front sitting room
where I could see the roses on the lawn from the wide and beautiful bay window, besides some of the ash and beech trees the old

Bailie had planted with his own hands when the mansion house was built. It meant that the trees were ninety-six years old.

The present James Ewan Booth is the third generation of the family in my lifetime, and it was his grandfather, James Cousins Booth I had come to talk about, the father and founder of the Downiehills story. Ewan's father, James David Booth had farmed the Dens estate, moving to the Home Farm of Downiehills when the old Bailie died, and I had known him also; but more intimately I had known his brother, Alexander Ewan Booth of Ednie, for whom I worked as cattleman for five years (1938–43).

While the genealogical tree was being sorted out I was introduced to Miss Susan Booth of the fourth generation and only child of the household, though now over twenty. Susan had just entered in a pale green trouser suit and I got up from the leather upholstery to greet her, the Booth features quite prominent in her country girl complexion. She takes an active interest in the family business and has a University degree in Business Law. At the moment she is pursuing a career in the tough sport of Eventing, which has something to do with horses and pony riding. Regrettably Ewan and Joan do not have a son to perpetuate the family name.

Our coffee finished and our cigarettes alight I began my research with Ewan.

It all began on 27 December 1856 when James Cousins Booth was born in Peterhead to Jonathan Booth, a whale-ship's carpenter, and Margaret Cousins of the same town. The father died when James was but ten years old and he had to leave school to fend for his widowed mother and sister Mary Ann.

He tried every coopering yard in Peterhead in search of a job but without success. Everywhere the answer was the same: 'Ye're owre young laddie, come back in a year or twa and we'll mabee gie ye a job.' But young Booth had to get a job now, so on the Saturday evening before closing time he made a round of the shops to see if any of them wanted a message boy. But there were no vacancies, and if there had been they said he was too young anyway. He deliberately avoided the butchers' shops because he didn't want to become a butcher, but when he had been turned away everywhere else he decided to give them a try. And sure enough, where he had least desired it, he was armed with a broom and shovel and was told to sweep out the shop and the pavement outside. It was a butcher's shop in Ellis Street near the harbour and on the Monday morning he began working full-time. The proprietor later moved to Broad Street and took young Booth with him and taught him the tricks of the trade. Seven years later his master retired and the young Booth of seventeen took over the business on his own.

He presented himself in the office of the factor for the property, Mr W C MacBean and calmly told him he wanted to take over the shop. MacBean apparently knew the young lad's qualities for after a few shrewd questions he allowed James Cousins Booth as the new proprietor to sign on the dotted line. So the young assist-ant became the young master, greatly to the chagrin of the foreman butcher, who had harboured similar ideas of his own, but had indulged in that fateful hesitancy which is so often detri-mental to progress. It was the first time but certainly not the last that Mr Booth would shrewdly forestal his competitors.

But for all his scraping and saving and denying himself the smallest luxuries of life the young butcher was short of hard cash. Night shift work was the only answer, working harder than when he was a paid servant to repay bank interest and replenish the shop with fresh meat and vegetables and pay his wage bill for his assistants.

He contracted with other butchers in the town to do a share of their slaughtering at an agreed sum per hour. This meant a great deal of hard night work, as well as eident days serving in the shop, but he 'wasna fear't at hard wark', and he was strong and determined now that he knew where he was going in the butchery trade. Physically too he was developing manfully, tall and broad-shouldered with head erect; easily picked out in a crowded sale ring, as he was in the showyards in later life, especially after he donned his everyday suit of black and white dam-brod squares, grey bowler hat and florid tie, when every-body in Buchan referred to him as 'Tartan Jim'. Ewan tells me that he joked with his friends about his suits being bought at the 'Fifty-Shilling Tailors', but he thinks they were of the Montague Burton cut and far more expensive. In middle life he is remem-bered as a striking and flamboyant figure, Dickensian almost, sartorial and dandified, with a 'Micawber' wit that matched the image and a shrewd sense of humour that could blunt the edge of serious issues. He may have seemed ostentatious but in manner he was disarming rather than aggressive and made friends everywhere, except perhaps in close business circles where he could be dogmatic or charming to meet the needs of the moment. In speech he could be at academic level on municipal benches but he never lost his Mither Tongue for the man in the street or for the ploughmen in his own parks.

But we must go back to the days when the young Jim Booth still wore his butcher's apron and could whet his knives behind the counter with mystifying slickness and dexterity, at the same time 'newsing up' his 'wifie' customers with accustomed familiarity in the role of family butcher. It was the day he discovered from the books that he had one-hundred pounds sterling clear profit from trading over a certain period; the day he felt confident to go out to the country and buy his own cattle direct from the farmers, cutting out the dealers who were giving him a rough time.

So he hung up his apron for good and became more managerial in his affairs. He later employed a certain Miss Birnie as his secretary and accountant and she remained in his employment for the rest of her long working life. He put on his best suit (not the tartan one yet) fixed a fresh flower for his buttonhole (which he still did in his eighties) and set forth in a hired gig on the West Road from Peterhead. It was polled cattle he was after, of the highest quality, and he was fortunate in calling on an old farmer who herded a good breed of cattle and who knew the value of ready cash. So the young butcher got the wyle o' the byre and became an exclusive customer, the farmer henceforth denying all others a purchase until 'young Booth had had his pick.' He also bought poultry from the farmer's wife after he had had his cup of tea.

By the 1870s young Booth was well established, but then ensued a depressive trading period in which he had to struggle among his competitors to survive, relying mainly on reserve capital which he hoped would carry him through. Then the bottom fell out of the Smithfield market and prices were so depressed that farmers everywhere were holding on to their fat cattle in the hope of a rise. The stalemate became serious as the weeks passed: byres filled with prime cattle and fodder and human food getting scarce and the agents at their wits' end. But almost instinctively Booth knew before most others when the tide would turn and he decided to gamble his all, win or lose. This time he fixed a carnation in his buttonhole and hired a phaeton and driver from Jamie Reid of the Royal Bazaar, because he didn't want to be distracted by having to drive a shelt around the Buchan countryside. His intention was to buy up all the fat cattle within a day's radius of Peterhead; everything within hail of his phaeton, and with all he possessed invested in the gamble his pocket-book was bulging at the seams. At the price he offered Booth had no difficulty in persuading the farmers to sell, and on returning home at night-fall he wondered seriously if he had bitten off more than he could chew. He later admitted to having spent one of the few sleepless nights of his long career, but in the morning he was heartened by a telegram informing him that Smithfield had recuperated and was commissioning him to buy *ad lib* for his London connections. His gamble had succeeded and his future was assured.

'That day', he said, 'you could not have hired a machine of any kind for love or money. All the dealers and butchers were out from daybreak, but everywhere they met the same tale: 'Too late, Booth bocht them a' yesterday.' He often described this as the biggest one-day single-handed cattle deal on record. After that it was a gradual but sure transition to Downiehills and the Bailie Booth whom the wider world knew so well.

On 28 June 1881 Mr Booth married Susan Ewan, daughter of a whaling captain who lived in Polar House, Peterhead, at the corner of Port Henry Road and Gladstone Road, which is still standing, and the ships captained by Mr Ewan were the *Windward* and *Polar Star*. Seven years later the Booths bought the farm of Downiehills, and after Mr Booth built the new farmhouse they moved out from Peterhead and spent their long lives together and brought up their family at Downiehills. The only blight on this period of their lives was the death of two of their children in infancy, Susan and Ewan Booth.

For over a hundred years the name of Booth had been on the board over the butcher's shop in Peterhead's Broad Street. The family sold the shop in 1962 but trade was carried on under the family name by the succeeding purveyor; not until 1983 when the

property again changed hands was the name of Booth removed
when the latest occupant decided to trade under his own name.
The name of Booth was synonymous with Peterhead's butcher
trade almost to the equivalence of Lord Boothby's name in the
town's political affairs, and it is significant that it was Bailie
Booth who initiated Boothby on his first ascendancy as a Tory
candidate for East Aberdeenshire, as I have recorded elsewhere.*

But by the time the name of Booth had been removed from
the shop-front the Bailie's grandson, son of James Booth of Dens,
the present Ewan Booth, had, by means of his refrigeration vans
given the name of Booth a new national importance, carrying it
deep into England in bold display.

After all, the Bailie once told 'Erchie' Campbell, known from
his literary work as 'The Buchan Fairmer,' and father of Flora
Garry— that he was more English that Scotch. 'Man', he said,
'the funny thing is that I am more English than Scotch. My
forebears came from England two-hundred years ago, and one
of them was presented with a gold medal for his success in
teaching the farmers of this part of the world how to cultivate and
improve the heavy clay soil of the district. The Booths are English
at roots.' On which Erchie Campbell commented: 'It was then
that I saw in a flash the solution of something that had puzzled
me. It was the Englishman in him, even more than the inevitable
checked suit and grey bowler which made him stand out as somehow different in any gathering of his Buchan compeers.'

He also told Erchie about the time before the days of anaes-
thetic when he visited a dentist to have a molar tooth extracted.
It was such a tussle over an hour in duration that the dentist took
a week in bed to recover from it. And it was 'so damned sair'
that the Bailie never visited a dentist again in his life.

'Ah, but he could tell stories,' said Ewan, when I related this,
and at this stage of our discussion I asked him if his refrigeration
venture could be in any way connected with the initiative and
endeavour of his pioneering grandfather?

His reply was inconclusive in that although his grandfather
had been in the meat trade and had bought Downiehills and
associated farms, the idea of refrigerated meat distribution was
entirely his own. 'I jist wanted a new line in business. A new

*A Chiel Among Them.

trade. I wanted tae branch oot. The estates are separate noo: Graham (his cousin, Graham Booth) farms Ednie and I have Downiehills. For family reasons we sold the Dens estate after my father died, but last year I bocht Mountpleasant, jist owre the hedge ye micht say, so I wasna losin' interest or grun, I jist wanted a new line o' business. We dinna fatten beasts for wir ain use, we jist sell dead weight like abody else.'

I took another sip of my coffee and continued with my notes.

Bailie Booth was only thirty-two years of age when he bought the estate of Downiehills in 1888. It was a dour clay hole with a derelict brickworks in the middle and the farm buildings had been sadly neglected over many years. But with the inherited skill of his ancestors in agriculture and the will and determination he had exercised in the meat trade, it wasn't many years or the future Bailie had transformed Downiehills from a morass of bulrush and croaking frog to an oasis in bloom.

Under Government subsidy for the old sole and tile drainage pipes he had drains dug and laid five yards apart and four feet deep all over the farm (which were the conditions of the grant) and despite the fact that the pipes were only two inches in diameter they may still be running water, just as the old stone drains are capable of doing. The Bailie had ditches dug to take the drains and built some ten miles of drystone dykes, most of which are still standing. He planted trees and hedges as shelter belts for cattle. To fertilise the land he had a ten-year contract with the Peterhead Town Council to drive toon's muck and slaughterhouse offal to Downiehills where he had middens all over the place. He built the mansion house around 1898 at a cost of £1,300, complete with bathroom plumbing and electric lighting generated on the premises. The architect was a Mr Clyne of Aberdeen. The steading also was renovated with suitable byres for cattle fattening with appropriate fodder barns and turnip sheds, stables, hay and grain lofts and cart and implement sheds. Some of the cottars were housed in the old 'Red Raw' of tiled cottages which had been attached to the defunct brickworks, but Bailie Booth built two more cottages at the end of the farm road leading up to Tortorston School. The cost was £40 a piece at the turn of the century.

Mrs Booth came forward with an enlargement of the family taken on the front steps of the mansion house in 1900. This was

before the days of the natty suit and the picture contained father
and mother and daughters Margaret, Mary Alice and Florabell;
sons James, Alexander and John, the latter emigrating to
Canada in 1913, where he died in 1934. Like Ewan, his cousin
(Uncle John's grandson) is also in road haulage in Canada, and
has a married sister in Glasgow.

With the family firmly established at Downiehills perhaps the
time is ripe to trace the history of the estate. In the old spelling it is Duniehills and is first mentioned in mid sixteenth
century when Lady Keith of Inverugie willed the lands of Duniehills to her nephew of Ravenscraig Castle, possibly of the Cheyne
family. It appears again in the Sasine Roll of 1630, referring
to legal possession of feudal property, when a famous family
of the name of Robertson had Sasine of the lands of Duniehills
for one hundred years. In the Valuation Roll of 1667 Thomas
Robertson is still in possession, with Sarah Robertson his spouse.
In the List of Pollable Persons within the Shire of Aberdeen in
1696, Duniehills is still belonging to Thomas Robertson, in all
probability a successor of the aforesaid, but with a subsidiary
income as 'minister of Longsyde and his familie living ther.'
Living in Duniehills is 'James Gordone, and Jean Robertson
his spouse (obviously a daughter of the minister) with their
daughter Jean Gordone and servants Wm Rickart, Alex Lillie
and Marjorie Matthew, with Paul Mackie cottar ther with wyfe
Janet Davison; James Elrick shoemaker and his wyfe Isobell
Craighead, Alexander Will, weaver, with Elizabeth Craik his
spouse, and Margaret Clerk, liveing by herself. Thomas Robertson, Lerd.'

After the 'Forty-five Rebellion Duniehills passed from the
Jacobite Keiths to the Fergusons of Pitfour, and at the time of
Bailie Booth's purchase was tenanted by a family of the name of
Will, who apparently had been unable to sustain the farm in a
cultivated state.

In 1908 Booth purchased the estate of Dens, comprising over
1,000 acres, including the Home Farm of Dens, Berryden and
Denholm as the principal farms, with several ancillary crofts.
Dens was first occupied by Alex Booth, the second son when he
married Anne Guthrie in 1916, and their family were all born
there: Moira, Guthrie, Graham and Vera. The Bailie bought the
Ednie estate in 1922 and Alex and his family moved there in

the same year when his elder brother married and went to Dens. James David Booth (JD) married Miss Margaret Skinner of Cortiebrae farm Lonmay and their family was also born at Dens. The present James Ewan Booth was born to them in 1924, followed by his four sisters, Margaret, Jean, Mary and Elizabeth.

Ednie comprised another 1,000 acres or so and was also purchased from the representatives of the now ailing Ferguson Estates of Pitfour. Besides the Home Farm of Ednie the acreage contained the farms of Little Ednie, South Kinloch, Bruxiehill, Corehill and several crofts where the steadings have crumbled and their names have been forgotten in the scheme of things. A most gracious bay-window frontage was added to the existing mansion house at Ednie, and Mid Essie Croft, St Fergus was later added to the estate.

James D Booth farmed Dens until his father died in 1940 and then moved to Downiehills. JD died at the age of seventy-two in 1955 and the present Ewan took over. The estate of Ednie was willed to Alex Booth when the old Bailie died. Alex farmed it until his death in 1955 when it fell to his sons, Guthrie and Graham. Guthrie Booth moved to Whiteside of Alford and Graham now farms Ednie, thus the estates now form two separate units, Ewan Booth at Downiehills and Graham Booth at Ednie. Family liability compels these changes and for similar reasons Ewan Booth disposed of the Dens estate when he became proprietor of Downiehills, though he has since replaced it with the acquisition of the neighbouring lands of Mountpleasant at Inverugie. Guthrie Booth has now retired from farming and lives in Grantown-On-Spey. He is the only one of all the Old Bailie's descendants who has a grandson to perpetuate the name of Booth.

But back to the grand old man of Downiehills, the Bailie and father of the family, who around 1890 established a herd of pedigree Aberdeen-Angus cattle which won him considerable success in the showyards. His most notable triumph was achieved at the Highland and Agricultural Society's Show at Inverness in 1923, when his seven-year-old cow, Erica of Downiehills (Cat. No. 57775) won the female championship and the Ballindalloch Cup. Ten years later in 1933, the Bailie was appointed President of the Aberdeen-Angus Cattle Society, a position he held for the next two years. But it was as a breeder and feeder of commercial cattle rather than as a breeder of pedigree stock that the Bailie excelled. He was one of the most extensive feeders of carcass meat cattle in the country; and he also kept a flock of over 1,000 Cheviot ewes and bred and fed large numbers of sheep for the wool and mutton trades.

The Bailie was also a prominent breeder of Clydesdales, so now we know from where the young Susan Booth of Downiehills has inherited her flair for saddle sports and her love for horses. Her great-grandfather liked a good horse, and the work horses on his extensive farms were mostly mares, kept for breeding as well as for working. He claimed to have bred more Clydesdale foals than anyone else in the county. Most of his foals commanded high prices and some of them attained showyard distinction. The Clydesdale gelding, 'Bellringer', a Royal Show Champion, was bred by the Bailie, and he also bred the well-known stallion, 'The Bailie', Cat. No. 20930. In recognition of his support of the Clydesdale breed Bailie Booth was one of the guests of honour at the dinner of the Northern Counties Affiliated Clydesdale Breeders at Aberdeen in 1927, on which occasion it was stated that although he had not made a fortune out of his Clydesdales, they had always paid their way as the best always do, and that none of them had left him in debt. Some of this 'horse sense' rubbed off on his son Alex, of Ednie, whom I have heard described as the best judge of horses in the Booth family, though not officially, and local opinion had it that Jim of Dens was best for cattle but that Alec had the best eye for a horse.

Cattle judging was another faculty in which the Bailie excelled, and for his discernment and fairness at these competitions he was highly respected. His varied experience and word wisdom carried such weight among his contemporaries it was inevitable that his services as a judge of livestock should be extensively called upon. In the judging ring his figure was one of the most familiar at cattle shows all over the country; tall, erect and dignified, with a keen eye for the classic qualities in an animal in making his decision for an award. In 1920 he had the honour of judging the Aberdeen-Angus cattle section at the great Palermo Show in Buenos Aires. His judgement and upstanding personality on that occasion resulted in his being invited a second time to adjudicate in the Argentine, at the Palermo Show of 1929.

On returning home the Bailie was entertained at a compli-
mentary dinner by the Deer branch of the Scottish Farmers'
Union, when tributes were showered on him by Mr Robert (now
Lord) Boothby MP, and by many others for his eminent services
to agriculture, at home and in Argentina.

In his long career the Bailie had been for a term President of
the Royal Northern Agricultural Society; the Aberdeen-Angus
Cattle Society; the Buchan Agricultural Society, and the Deer
branch of the Farmers' Union. It appears that his neighbours and
friends took special delight in honouring him, and it was a mark
of esteem that represented more than admiration. It reflected a
gratitude for the readiness and kindliness in which the Bailie
placed the fruits of his wide experience at the disposal of young
farmers, when his advice to beginners in the practice of farming
was exemplary and practical and vastly encouraging.

It has been said of him that 'he was an even better judge of
a man than of a beast', and that that was a great asset in his
favour; for, having measured his man accurately, 'he had an
infallible gauge upon all his future dealings with him.'

Here again I am greatly indebted to the late Archibald
Campbell (Erchie) an astute observer of the Bailie in his day,
and I beg to quote from his obituary notice for his late friend
in the Buchan Observer for 31 December 1940. 'The better one
got to know the Bailie the more one was surprised by his versatility. In everything he undertook he had the acknowledged
touch of the master. As a raconteur he had few equals, and he
could give point to every story with a few appropriate touches of
accurate local lore . . . In later years he wrote several passable
songs, adjusted them to suitable tunes, and could sing them with
agreeable effect. He had the gift of compounding proverbial
sayings into which he compressed a wisdom that often cut deeper
than that of the pundits. He retained to the last an infectious
boyishness. It broke through in his smile, and in his quick eye
to the amusing idiosyncrasies of others. He liked to describe
himself as one who had been a showman all his life, but he was
always sufficiently guileless to take an eager interest in the effect
of his performance.

James Scott Skinner, the Strathspey King, composed a tune
in his honour, 'The Bailie Booth Rant', a rousing compliment,
and the score is still extant at Downiehills.

Quoting from *Old Peterhead*, by Robert Neish (P Scrogie Ltd Peterhead, 1950) I give the following appreciation:

> Not only throughout Scotland, but to the most remote corners of the earth, the 'kenspeckle' figure of Bailie Booth was well known. His death removed one of the most familiar characters of his day . . . Free from affectation, gentle and unassuming, his manly frame enshrined a heart of sterling worth. A son of the open spaces, Nature never failed to command his loyal devotion. He loved it in all its variant aspects with tender simplicity. The fleeting cloud, the golden grain, the wayside flower, the cattle in the fields, all touched something in the soul of the man, who was convinced that
>
> > All are but parts of one stupendous whole
> > Whose body Nature is and God the soul.
>
> Frequently the Bailie remarked that 'there wis naething in his heid bit beasts', but his friends and intimate acquaintances never accepted that valuation of his intellectual capabilities. His success in life was the direct result of his keen natural ability. His reputation as a leader of agriculture, and as a man of affairs, was firmly based upon force of character and carefully accumulated years of experience.

One can envisage a warm sunny autumn afternoon at the farm of Dens where there had been a cattle and crop demonstration, the mellowing stooks on the golden stubble fields and the russet leaves forming on the trees. The company had just finished a luxurious tea party on the lawn in front of the farmhouse and everybody was in high spirits, including the Bailie, who had acted as master of ceremonies, and now called for a song from a Devonshire farmer in their ranks, a request which was generously applauded and rendered in vigorous style 'a capital rollicking ballad redolent of the English soil.' But just to prove that all the musical talent was not confined to south of the border the Bailie then invoked a Turriff balladeer, a rich baritone, to give something in response, whereupon he sang a traditional Bothy Ballad with its characteristic lilting refrain. 'Now then,' cried the Bailie, 'we've sung the praises of the land, and I think we might have a verse or twa about the sea', and a young kinswoman of local repute gave a delightful rendition of 'The Tarrin' o' the Yoll'. Everybody was satisfied to call it a day, and all departed much the better of the cheerful influence of friendly, inspirational company. There were similar gatherings at Downiehills when occasion arose, and the guests were further enlivened by a game of croquet on the side lawn under the trees, the only physical game that the Bailie indulged in, and for sedentary relaxation in the winter evenings he liked playing whist with a few chosen friends.

In the twilight of his days his son James would take the old man in to Aberdeen when he went to the marts on a Friday. They would walk round the cattle pens and then take a seat at the ringside, where they would watch the sales and perhaps James would offer a bid for store cattle. They had dinner in the mart restaurant, after which James would return to the sales and leave the old man to his own wiles. He would take a bus to Union Street and walk along Diamond Street to the News Cinema. 'An Ideal Place for an Idle Hour', was the slogan of this delightful little cinema in the nineteen-thirties, and that's just what he did there, 'spent an idle hour,' though he was never a real film fan, and then he would have a cup of tea in the Palace Restaurant in Union Street and wait for his son to pick him up on the way home.

Despite the honour bestowed on him in 1929 it wasn't a year of triumph for the Bailie, or if it was it was tear-blurred for him by the loss of his dear wife, who was no longer there to share it. Susan Ewan died at the age of seventy-one and she was buried beside their little ones, Susan and Ewan in Landale Road Cemetery in Peterhead. The names Susan and Ewan have been family names since the young butcher met his future bride at Polar House in the days of the old whaling skipper. Ewan was Alex of Ednie's middle name and Ewan and daughter Susan are still very much alive at Downiehills.

The Bailie was seventy-three when his wife died, and for the next eleven years of his life he was looked after at Downiehills by his daughter Flora. By this time his son James of Dens was taking care of the butchery business and the Bailie became more desultory and relaxed in his activities. One of his last duties in the year before he died was with the wartime livestock department of the Ministry of Food Council, where his valuable advice and instruction earned him the warm thanks of the Ministry.

Much earlier in his life, and concurrent with his extensive farming enterprises, including the meat trade, the Bailie took a prominent part in the public affairs of the town of Peterhead. He was one of her most dutiful sons. Entering the Town Council in 1892 he held the office of Treasurer and was Senior Magistrate at the time of his retirement from civic duties. He was for many years a Feuars' Manager, rendering useful service as a County Councillor, was long a member and chairman of the Deer District Licensing Bench, and was a valued member of the East Aberdeenshire Unionist Association. He was a Justice of the Peace of Aberdeenshire, a director of various companies in Peterhead and district and he evinced a practical interest in the fishing and other local industries.

But despite all these multifarious activities the Bailie still had time to attend roup, market, show or kirk. Indeed he was a great kirk body, a devoted and lifelong member of St Peter's Church in Peterhead, where for sixty years he was a member of the vestry, serving for the greater part of that time as Chairman of the Vestry and Lay Elector. But for all his religious zeal and endeavour for the kirk he was not above stripping the ears of corn on a Sunday when unavoidable circumstances compelled him to slaughter, skin and debone a fat stot for the butcher shop on Monday morning. Perhaps he regarded it as a meat offering as prescribed in the Old Testament, the Blood of the Lamb; but no doubt if the local Pharisees had questioned him on the subject he would have had a ready answer for them.

It has also been said of the Bailie that he could sometimes be penny wise and pound foolish. When he had made a thousand pounds profit he would borrow ten thousand more to make a purchase, a rash gamble, though it usually paid off, yet he would hesitate at a roup when a second-hand binder went over £5 and withheld his bid—or did he just notice the crofter who was bidding against him and let the poor man have the machine? He also had featherbrained ideas like filling twelve-inch field drain pipes with cement as pillars without reinforcement to support the expansive roof of a cattle court. In the first gale of wind, even before the structure was complete, it collapsed like the proverbial pack of cards and was scattered all over the place. He was a rich man and could afford to spend money yet he seemed to find a sly humour in doing things on the cheap, like lean-to buildings to avoid building a wall, or damming up a ditch in place of a watering trough. The Bailie was indeed an enigma.

From the obituary notice for the Bailie I quote:

> Taken all in all the Bailie was pre-eminently one of those men who by appearance, personality and achievement are accorded by common consent a dominating place in their chosen spheres of action. He was recognised by his contemporaries as a leader, and his death leaves a gap which may not be soon or easily filled.

For sheer character alone I don't think the gap has ever really been filled. Circumstances have changed and there could never be another Bailie Booth, another colourful 'Tartan Jim' to enliven the imagination of the Buchan countryside.

Erchie Campbell continues:

> I give those glimpses of the progress of a self-made man to show that there was no facile luck about it. An almost unlimited capacity for hard work was the foundation of the Bailie's success. But hand-in-hand with that went an equally great capacity for self-denial, an unusual endowment of shrewd mother wit, much grit and determination, the cheerful disposition which comes from a clean mind and a healthy body, and one other quality which is not so easy to define. Perhaps I can best describe it as the gift of judgement—that faculty which causes a man to stand firmly by his own estimates and to find them in the main correct.

I remember him as a very old man when he used to visit Ednie in Jim's car with the present Ewan as a schoolboy in the back seat. Ewan remembered it too when I was head cattleman for his Uncle Alex at Ednie. Ewan and his father went into the farmhouse, but the old man came to the byre for a smoke of his pipe, perhaps because he didn't like smoking it in the house, and forbye, he could have a news with another baillie, the cattleman. He still wore his checked suit and grey hat and buttonhole, although it was like himself by now a bit 'peelie-wallie', drooping like his moustache, maybe because he had forgotten to change it from the day before. Anyway I had a stirk a bit under the weather and he asked what was wrong with it. The beast was standing back from his food at the full length of his neck chain, head down, ears drooping, back slightly arched and his tail held firm between his hind legs.

'Is his lugs caul'?' the Bailie asked. I assured him that they were. 'Ye shid tak' a' his maet oot in front o' 'im cattleman. Leave 'im wi' a teem troch. Mabee he jist needs a dose o' salts and black treacle. Man,' he continued, 'ye can ie tell fin a beast's nae weel if his lugs are caul', or if he's nae chawin' the queed, or ootside if he's staunin' a' by himsel' in the neuk o' a park.' When the Bailie had gone we gave the animal a dose of the recommended salts and treacle and in a day or two he recovered his appetite but had skittered from the purgation.

Of course I had seen the Bailie before, when he came to watch the weaning of the lambs, and for three nights we couldn't get sleep for heart-broken thirsty lambs bleating round our cottages near the loading pens. He also came at silage time when most of the men from Dens and Berryden and Downiehills came across the Ugie river to assist us with greencrop tares and beans. There was never a word from his head cattleman until the old Bailie appeared and then he was in his element. The two of them got together and the diatribe that ensued between them brought smiles from all within earshot. That a man of the municipal rostrum could engage in such humorous drivel with his servant was just unbelieveable, and the things that the servant said to his master I wouldn't have dared mention to anyone I ever worked for, and I'm doubtful if any of the others would have got away with it. But the man had been a trusted servant of the Bailie for nearly half-a-century and knew his every mood and how to cajole him into such tomfoolery. But the man was merely boosting his own ego because he was a bit hen-pecked at home, and if he could be heard on such familiar terms with the Bailie in the presence of others it tilted his windmill to catch the breeze and he enjoyed it. The Bailie knew all this and perhaps appeased the man. He also knew that the man wasn't allowed to smoke in his own home, but had to go furth to the gairden for a blow at his pipe, or into a shed in a cold night. He didn't care for the wife either who milked his kye at Downiehills. When she took her pails out of the milkhouse she clashed and clanged and clattered among them intentionally to such an extent that she had the household awake much earlier than they would have preferred.

Mrs Booth offered me lunch, which I humbly declined on the excuse that I had a sandwich and tea in the car and further research to be completed in the library at Peterhead while I was in the area, whereupon she reluctantly released me into the sunshine which was streaming down on the verdant policies of Downiehills. We walked round the manion house and after a stroll in the garden I got in the car and said farewell to my hosts on the driveway.

On leaving Downiehills I had lunch in the car park at Finefare Stores on the west fringe of Peterhead. Then I slipped into town and parked in Prince Street, from where I walked to the Arbuthnott Library and the editorial offices of the Buchan Observer. Coming out of town I searched for and found the Booth Memorial Headstone in the Landale Road Cemetery where I copied down all the particulars of bereavement, which are added here for those who are interested.

There remains only the funeral, which was one of the largest ever seen in Peterhead, and but for wartime travelling restrictions would have been even larger, judging by the volume of condolences received by the Booth family.

St Peter's Church was filled at the impressive memorial service, conducted by Bishop Dean, assisted by the Rev E F Easson, rector of the church. As the cortege moved from St Peter's to the cemetery it was joined by a large number of mourners who couldn't get into the church.

The pall-bearers were sons Messrs J D Booth, Dens, and A E Booth, Ednie, and grandsons Ewan Booth, Dens, and Graham Booth, Ednie. (His brother Guthrie Booth was at this time a prisoner of war in Germany); G Connon, nephew, Peterhead; J M Thomson, Peterhead and Alf Reid, Aberdeen.

The occasion was graced by the presence of the Earl of Caithness, Convener of the county, and Colonel G B Duff of Hatton Castle, President of the East Aberdeenshire Unionist Association. Peterhead Town Council was represented by Bailie Work, senior magistrate; Mr Alex Davidson, town clerk; Councillor R S Dingwall and others. Mr William Hay, deputy-chairman, was among those representing the Peterhead Feuars' Managers.

Among representatives of agricultural bodies were: Mr D J Fowlie, Millhill, Longside; Mr John Strachan, Auchrynie, Mr J M Birnie, Longside; Mr Pat Strachan, Aberdeen; Mr F Milne,

Methlick; John Reith, Kennerty; Mr J Duthie Webster, Tarves; Mr Harry Milne, Fetterletter; Mr George Dalgarno, Rashboglea; and for the Auction Marts—Messrs Bryson Middleton, Aberdeen; John Duncan, Aberdeen; A E M Taylor, Mintlaw and John Webster, Maud.

Again I quote from Erchie Campbell's obituary

> For many a day none who knew the Bailie will pass Downiehills without sparing a thought for the man who is no longer there. To a larger extent than most men can claim of any place, he made that flourishing farm a pleasant abode. Most of the trees he planted with his own hand. He knew nearly every blade of grass in the lush fields. He was the personal enemy of every docken and thistle. In a very literal sense he WAS Downiehills.

On my way home I met another EWAN BOOTH refrigerator van in the Square at Ellon. I gave the driver a flash of my lights and he waved to me, because he is a nephew of my wife, Mr Michael Willox of Mintlaw, who has been in Mr Booth's service for a good many years. But I could swear he never guessed I had just come from Downiehills and an interview with his boss. I had had a full day.

IN MEMORIAM

ERECTED BY

James C Booth J P Downiehills
In Memory Of His Wife Susan Ewan
Who Died 5th January, 1929 Aged
71 Years. And His Two Children
Susan And Ewan`Who Died In Infancy.
His Mother Margaret Cousins Who Died
28th. March, 1895 Aged 69 Years. His
Sister Mary Ann Booth or Mathison, Who
Died 16th March, 1917 Aged 65 Years.
Also The Above James C Booth J P Who
Died 24th Dec. 1940 Aged 84 Years.
Also Margaret Brown Skinner, Beloved Wife
Of James D Booth, Who Died 8th March
1947, Aged 55 Years. The Above James D Booth,
J P Who Died 1st Nov. 1955 Aged 72 Years.
Flora Bell Booth Died 9th Nov. 1969 Aged
72 Years. Daughter Of The Above
James C Booth.

REST IN PEACE

DOCTOR BRUCE OF
INVERQUHOMERY

Of all the Buchan parishes Longside is one of my favourites,
perhaps because it was where I spent the springtime of my life,
or because the village and district has nurtured an esoteric few
who have left their names on the escutcheon of fame: Jamie
Fleeman, John Skinner of 'Tullochgorum' and Linshart, John
Imray, Peter Still, and now to my enlightened discovery, Dr
Alexander Bruce, LLD, MA, MD, FRCPE, FRSE, the Scottish
Father of Psychiatry. Even today, seventy-four years after his
death, his X-ray apparatus and electro-medical equipment can
still be viewed in the British Museum, and samples of his printed
works on neurology can be consulted in the medical archives of
Edinburgh University. Besides his private practice he held fourteen appointments as pathologist and physician at Edinburgh
Infirmary, consulting on subjects like Lymphatics of the Spinal
Cord, Cerebral Tumour and Haemorrhage, Spinal Paralysis,
Muscular Atrophy, Meningitis, and many other kindred subjects. He wrote three books on neurology and translated two
others, and in conjunction with other scholars left some forty-
five papers on diseases of the nervous system, syphilitic infection
and diabetes. Epilepsy, my own complaint, would have been
understood by Dr Bruce of Inverquhomery, just across the fields
from Nether Kinmundy but that he died two years before I was
born.

The parish of Longside is almost hymnal in its pastoral serenity, where the pastures are fresh and the waters are musical, and the avenues of trees, like the 'Belts of Ludquharn, soften the land-scape into sylvan splendour. The 23rd psalm comes alive for me at Longside and symbolises my contentment with the environ-ment. A great many of my friends lie buried at Longside, and the origin of my pen-name is etched on a gravestone visible from the gate at the new cemetery, on the road to Ludquharn. The name of Charles Tolmie, a crofter from Rora, prefixed with David in place of Charles, was misprinted as Toulmin by a feckless compositor and has remained with me these forty years. It is the parish where the Lamp of Knowledge was first kindled in my soul.

From the cemetery gates at Longside I can still see the cottage with the tree at the gable at Nether Kinmundy, and the modern-ised steading where I laboured in the byres with my father, and the pleasant fields and hedgerows where I worked in a euphoria of budding culture and a heady awakening to the joy of partici-pation in the arts, mostly sketching and painting at that stage, before I was ripe for the pen. It was where I caught the magic of the cinema and got tuned-in to Tin Pan Alley on my father's gramophone—where I first listened to the accordion music of William Hannah, the Cornkisters of Willie Kemp and G S Morris, and the monologues of Dufton Scott; yet never dreaming that I shared the utopia of former poets and scholars, embracing literature, music, religion and medical science, the latter in the person of Dr Alexander Bruce of Inverquhomery.

The name of Inverquhomery (like Balquhindachy at Methlick) and how to pronounce it is sometimes a euphonic conundrum for visitors to Longside, until they hear the inhabitants give it as 'Innerfummery,' a simplification which makes the Gaelic erse sound like an easy language. Inver means mouth and the farm stands above the mouth of the Quhomery Burn where it enters the river Ugie, thus Inverquhomery. It is the wooded Home Farm on an eminence south of the village, distinguished by its stately manor house and three cone-shaped dovecots over the prison-like garden walls. It is approached from the village by the 'Swan's Neck' road from near the Lych Gate at the Parish Kirk and the burial vault of the Bruces. But there is a distinction about the name scarcely realised by the modern inhabitants of Longside, although some of the older folks can recall the last 'Lairdie' and members of his family. It was his father who pioneered the study of psychiatry and neurology and multiple sclerosis long before those names became known in our common language. Even in my own youth at Longside about the only thing I knew of Inverquhomery was that there they had the biggest bucket water-wheel in Buchan for driving the threshing mill, seventeen feet in diameter, and that the second largest of sixteen-feet was at Newton of Kinmundy.

There have been Bruces at Inverquhomery for over two hundred years, from the mid seventeenth century to mid twentieth century. Their ancestry has been traced from Ninian Bruce of Newseat of Peterhead, who died around 1699, and whose grandson, Alexander Bruce, settled at Inverquhomery. James Bruce, grandson of Alexander, born 1785, purchased the estates of Inverquhomery and Longside from Mr George Ferguson of Pitfour in 1827. James Bruce made a fortune in shipping at Peterhead, and was a Magistrate and Commissioner of Supply for Aberdeenshire. His brother Alexander farmed Millhill on the Kinmundy estate, owned by a branch of the Pitfour Fergusons and marching with Inverquhomery. Alexander had two sons, James and Alexander, junior and when their uncle at Inverquhomery died in 1862, James inherited his estate. Alexander, junior, married Miss Mary Milne, daughter of William Milne of Ardendraught in Cruden, and settled as tenant farmer of Ardiffery, in the same parish. It is therefore the Millhill branch of the family we are at present concerned with, until Inverquhomery came to them on the death of the incumbent James in 1900. But we will catch up again with that later in our chronicle.

Meanwhile we must revert to Alexander Bruce of Cruden, and his wife Mary Milne. The couple were married on 18 October 1853, and on 16 September the next year a son was born to them, their only child, again Alexander Bruce, later Dr Alexander Bruce of Inverquhomery and Edinburgh, the main subject of our discussion.

PARENTAGE

Dr Bruce's parents were both quite remarkable people and highly respected by all who shared their acquaintance. His father was one of the most prominent and enterprising tenant farmers in Aberdeenshire, a distinction which became more widely apparent when he moved to the larger farm of Millhill on the death of his father in 1862, just over the dyke from Inverquhomery. Alexander Bruce of Millhill was what we might regard nowadays as a practical and progressive farmer, anxious to experiment and improve upon all aspects of agriculture, from the application of the then 'new' chemical fertilisers to grass and animal husbandry, the propagation of new crop varieties and improved methods of cultivation. When he died in 1885 the *Peterhead Sentinel* reported of him:

> One of the largest farmers on the Kinmundy Estate, Mr Bruce was widely known in the north as an energetic and enterprising agriculturist, shrewd and intelligent in his business, keenly alive to every movement likely to assist the cause of agriculture, and thoroughly abreast of the age in its scientific aspect and in all matters which should be important to the practical farmer . . . He was Vice-President of the Buchan Agricultural Society, and took a keen interest alike in its exhibitions (in which he himself was not seldom a successful exhibitor with his fine herd of Shorthorn cattle), and in the discussions which from time to time took place on agricultural topics at the dinners and other gatherings, where his happy good humour always rendered him exceedingly popular . . . Not a fluent or ready speaker, he was nevertheless an exceedingly well-read and well-informed man on many subjects. A fellow of the Royal Antiquarian Society, he took a special interest in antiquarian studies and he had a keen taste for art, specimens of which he avidly collected. In politics, he was a staunch and ardent Conservative, and took no little interest in the organisation of that party in the north. Lately he had taken much interest in the formation of the curling club at Pitfour, in which he had enrolled himself a member, and was taking part in the game with great zest only a few days before his death. In many other relations, he came much in contact with all classes in Buchan, and was everywhere popular, and his genial face and portly figure were familiar at most of the important agricultural shows in the north. In many circles his hearty vigour and unfailing bonhomie will be greatly missed.

Doctor Bruce's mother, Mary Milne, has also been remarked upon as a capable and ingenious woman who was very popular with all her friends and neighbours, and very generous and considerate to her servants inside and out of the farmhouse. The story is told of her while at Ardiffery of how she managed to cope with an accident in harvest time which would have proved most embarrassing for a woman of lesser spirit or inventiveness. It concerned the harvest dinner, served at noon, a great pot of tattie-soup hung (suspended) under the axle of a horse cart and conveyed to the hairst rigs, where all forgathered from reaper and sheaf binding to partake thereof in the lithe of a stook. On this particular day, swinging under the showdin' cart, the bow of the heavy pot broke and all the fine hot soup was spilled on the stubble. Consternation reigned among the hungry workers and news of the disaster was conveyed to Mrs Bruce by one of the servants. But she rose to meet the emergency and boiled another pot of 'saps', breadcrumbs boiled in milk and sweetened, and, to silence the critics, added a good jelp from the whisky pig. The loss was soon made good, and what with oat-cakes forbye, the lads in their nicky-tams declared that they 'wouldna mind gin the bow o' the pot broke ilka day!' Her kindness to the servants of both sexes was proverbial and she was well-liked by them all. In the words of a friend: 'Mrs Bruce was the soul of generosity, not only in material matters, but to the faults and failings in others. To do a kindly action she regarded as a privilege and joy.'

SCHOOLDAYS

The farm of Ardiffery in Cruden, where Dr Bruce was born, lies in the shelter of the brae to the west of the Parish Church of St Olaf, near the Bishop's Brig. The soil is a rich loam lustered with red clay and the situation slopes gently south to catch the sun, while the breeze from sea or moorland is always pleasantly sweet. In wilder mood the climate is vigorously healthy and the young boy throve in this alternately mild and boisterous environment. But he was only a child of seven and newly started school when in 1862 his parents moved from Cruden to Millhill at Longside. From Millhill for a time he toddled over by Dury and Clola to the school at Shannas; later to Longside Secondary School and by the age of ten he was attending the Chanonry House School in Old Aberdeen—better known as the 'Gym' or Gymnasium, where he was boarded under the care of the Principal, Rev Dr Anderson, LLD, of St Andrew's University.

The 'Gym' was founded by Dr Anderson, 'Govie'. as the boys called him, probably because he used 'Govie Dick', as a swear word in trying circumstances; but at any rate some of the best brains in Aberdeen were first exercised within the precincts of his school, embracing French, German and Chemistry, prior to University training. The curriculum also included athletic exercises, of which the young Bruce was not an eager adherent. He remained there for six years and received a good basic training in all the subjects which suited him for a University career.

He was a diligent scholar and a favourite with his teachers, sometimes to the chagrin of his classmates, from whom he invoked taunts and criticism, especially when he found favour with the beautiful Annie Connell, a girl in the care of Mrs Anderson, the Principal's wife. His companions regarded Bruce as 'too bookish, very reticent, stand-offish and dour'. He seldom engaged in any of their games and referred to those who did as being 'all arms and legs' and inwardly may have added 'and no brains'. Yet they appointed him as captain of the school football club and he spoke of the benefit he derived from such healthy exercise. He was nick-named 'Cheese' after a stong-smelling kebbock had arrived for the Andersons from Mrs Bruce's dairy at Millhill farm. One boy wrote: 'Of course we all knew about his weakness for Annie Connell, and that may have kept us from giving him our confidence. It certainly made us merciless'. It may also have made them envious. The Principal, however, knew his worth, and always spoke of him with the utmost respect and reverence.

And who was this 'Flower of the Gym', the sweet and smiling Miss Connell? She was born in India, daughter of Lieutenant Connell, a native of Langholm in Dumfriesshire, but after the death of her father (her mother isn't mentioned) she was made a ward of Mrs Anderson at the now demolished 'Gym' school in Old Aberdeen. The boyish Bruce had a crush on the auburn-haired Annie from their first meeting and in manhood she became his wife.

Lieutenant Connell studied at the Royal Military College in Edinburgh. In 1846, having been appointed to the 1st regiment of Infantry, he sailed for India. Later he was given command of the Camel Corps. In 1848 he was engaged in the siege of Moult

Moultan and received a medal for his services. Shortly afterwards he was given a staff appointment as executive engineer in the Belgian Collectorate. His passion was big game hunting in the thickest jungles and he sent his Bengal tiger skins home to Langholm. His early death at twenty-five (perhaps from jungle fever) was deeply deplored. 'In India he left many friends and not a single enemy'. His daughter was soon afterwards sent to Scotland for her education.

UNIVERSITY LIFE

Bruce was an arduous, hard working student, as indeed he was a conscientious perfectionist throughout his working life. With consistent tenacity he endeavoured to research and develop every theory in the advancement of medical science, especially in the study of brain and nerve function and the structure of the spinal vertebrae and the relevant disorders affecting these organs. In October 1870, just after his sixteenth birthday, he became a student at Aberdeen University. He entered it as first bursar of his year and came through with flying colours. He really went up just to try the Bursary Examination, intending to compete in earnest the following year. Much to everybody's surprise however, he came out first and decided to proceed at once to the University. 'Only the Aberdonian of thirty years ago', wrote Sir Leslie MacKenzie in the *Lancet*, 'Can give that distinction its true meaning. To have a "first" at the "Comp" (the only real name of the Bursary Competition) was the ambition of every important schoolmaster in Aberdeenshire. It meant a career to the scholar.'

Out of a possible 1,200 marks, Bruce achieved 947. His nearest competitor had 922 marks and the third 909. These were the only three entrants who scored over 900. Bruce's marks for Latin and Greek were also exceptionally good. His English-Latin version scored 360 marks out of a possible 400, his Latin-English 123 out of 150, and his Greek paper 150 out of 175. In all 257 students competed, and of these 56 were placed. Bruce was assigned the Bursary of highest value—£35. Sir Leslie MacKenzie wrote: 'Success at the "Comp" was possible only to the capable classical boy, and Bruce was one of them.'

He maintained his high position in classics throughout the course. The Seafield Gold Medal for Latin fell to him, and the Simpson prize of £70 for Greek—'the blue ribbon of Classics at the University'. In other subjects he was almost equally brilliant, and at the end of his fourth year he was awarded the Town Council Gold Medal, a medal given to the most distinguished student of each year. Bruce's reputation in the Classics was of such high proficiency that his professors and fellow students expected that he would make a career of it. Bruce however had his own misgivings about the wisdom of such a career. The realms of high scholarship attracted him, but he was still more attracted by the appeal of a useful and practical life; the ideal of applied science as it appeared to him. He left Aberdeen and studied for three months in London with a posting in the Indian Civil Service in mind, but then returned to Edinburgh and took classes in Chemistry, Physics and Geology. From that time science claimed him, and the following year he became a regular student of Medicine at Edinburgh University. As one contemporary has it

> Fortunately for the science of Europe he preferred the richer new fields of medicine . . . He had the positive scientific mind, the sure-footedness of the born investigator, the unlimited capacity to make hypotheses, the faculty of exact analysis of data. Given these, a man will end in science, no matter what the bias of his literary studies may be.

As at Aberdeen, Bruce's courses at Edinburgh University was crowned with distinction. The hard-working Aberdonian was convincingly recognised over the four year period for the stuff he was made of. He gained the Grierson Bursary on entrance, and the Tyndal-Bruce Bursary at the end of his third session in 1878, and in his last year the much coveted Ettles Scholarship prize. He obtained the first place in the classes of Anatomy, Surgery (junior and senior), Practice of Medicine, Practical Gynaecology, Mental Diseases, and distinction in Physiology, Pathology etc. With such an outstanding record most men would have taken a breather, but not so Bruce—medal after medal followed, almost invariably first, whether junior or senior, in theoretical, laboratory, or clinical work, until he graduated MB and CM in 1879;

and for excellence in post-graduate clinical work he claimed the Leckie-Mactier Fellowship award, which secured him as a Bachelor of Medicine, the compounded interest of the sum of £2,000 over a period of three years.

Throughout these strenuous years our up and coming doctor managed to spend the furtive week-end and most of his Christmas and summer holidays on his father's farm at Millhill. He may also have visited at Inverquhomery, at that time occupied by his eccentric uncle, James Bruce Esquire, his father's brother, who had a childless marriage with a Miss Diana Wheeler, and had made a fortune from his shipping interests in Peterhead.

Now in his twenty-fifth year it is also supposed that the young doctor had by now presented Miss Annie Connell at Millhill and introduced her to his parents. The young couple would arrive by train at Longside station, where the Terrace gardens were glowing with daffodils, dusty millers, tulips and lubellia; the white and pink cherry trees a froth of blossom, while chestnut, beech and lime trees unfolded their fresh new leaves in the greenery of summer. Mr Bruce and his strapper (groom) would be waiting for them with the phaeton, and after a hearty welcome the party would drive over the railway bridge and the Ugie and along the haughs into the village; up the Inn Brae by the kirk, down by the school and manse and up through the Belts of Ludquharn, over by Clayhills and down by Old Mill farm over the bridge and up the steep brae to Millhill, where Mrs Bruce would have a hot meal waiting for them and the kindest of welcomes.

ON THE CONTINENT

Back in harness in Edinburgh Bruce pursued a course in post graduate study in medicine of the most thorough and exhaustive nature. During the three years in which he was to benefit financially from the Leckie-Mactier Fellowship award he was obliged to attend examinations and give written reports and commentaries on medical, surgical and gynaecological cases in the University wards of Edinbugh Royal Infirmary, accompanied by written examinations in midwifery, Medical Jurisprudence, and on Public Health. Every holder of the Fellowship during his tenure had to transmit his experiences in writing, and, if required, read publicly in the presence of the Medical Faculty a communication embodying the result of original observation or historical research in some department of medicine.

To gain practical experience on these matters Bruce acted for three months as clinical assistant to Bevan Lewis at the West Riding Asylum, Wakefield, which was considered 'a school for many distinguished neurologists'. Lewis was really the first to inspire him to make a special study of the brain, and under Lewis's guidance he spent most of his spare time during these months in studying modern methods of examining diseased conditions of the nervous system. He spent a further year as resident physician in the Royal Infirmary, Edinburgh, after which time he went abroad to study in Vienna, Heidelberg, Frankfurt and Paris. At Vienna he worked on diseases of the eye under Fuchs, of the ear under Gruber and Polizer; of the nervous system, of the throat and of the chest under Schroter and Chiari, surgery under Billroth, syphilis under Fingar, and gynaecology in the wards of the Allgemeines Krankenhaus in the Josefstadt. 'Comprehensive though the plan of work was', wrote one commentator on Bruce, 'no part of it was done in a slipshod or perfunctory fashion. German lessons taken from Keihaupt occupied his mind as completely when engaged on them as did his studies on the nervous system. Concentration, promptness and perseverance were then, as to the end, the chief characteristics of Bruce's method and work.'

But all work and no play makes Jack a dull boy, as they say, so there had to be some diversion in the city of the Blue Danube and the Straus Waltzes, opera and the fashion ballrooms, and in the romantic aura associated with Vienna. Sir Sims Woodhead, who was then a fellow student with Bruce has left us a written account of their stay in the City of Dreams, which is sensibly alternated with studious pursuit and recreation.

Bruce and I kept together in Vienna where, naturally, we had many interests and pursuits in common. We had with us a number of introductions, not only to Professors, but to others. Many of the other Edinburgh men, some twenty in number, obtained similar introductions, but, apparently, did not present them as they wished to be as free as possible to go and come, and to have no ties that might interfere with their work or excursions. Bruce and I, wishing to see something of the home life of our Viennese hosts, presented these introductions; and I need scarcely say that Bruce was PERSONA GRATA to all with whom he came in contact. His interest in everything that was going on, his self-contained but cheery manner and buoyant spirits, gained the favour of all; and I can never be sufficiently grateful for the fact that I was associated with him. At the end of our sojourn all agreed that we had chosen the better part; for we came to the conclusion that our Viennese hosts must have suspected that not we alone had been provided with introductions, for they made every effort to show us that our confidence in their hospitality was not a vain thing. Invitations to suppers, concerts, the opera, club balls—it was carnival time—poured in on us; and much private hospitality was tendered. It really appeared as though these good people were anxious to show our colleagues what they had missed by not availing themselves of the opportunities afforded them by their introductions; and those who knew Bruce can well imagine how he used to chuckle as taking our meals at Lintzenmeyer's, he would pawkily suggest that 'perhaps they had something better on' than some gorgeous entertainment to which we had been bidden. I can honestly say, however, that none of this entertainment was allowed to interfere with the main object of our visit to Vienna though it rendered that visit very much more enjoyable and in many ways more profitable.

Another student commentator of those days was Dr Vincent Bowditch of Boston USA, who also shared in their studies and revels. He speaks of gaining in Vienna through his fellowship with Bruce,

> many memories not only of strenuous and inspiring labours, but of pleasant interludes, of social functions enjoyed, of real friendships made and cemented—memories which stand out as red-letter records in even the brightest periods of life.

At Frankfurt Bruce came under the spell of Professor Weigert, who greatly helped him in his studies of the central nervous system.

MARRIAGE AND SOCIAL LIFE

On 22 December 1881, after his return from mainland Europe, Bruce was married to Miss Annie Louisa Connell, his boyhood sweetheart, at Hilton House, Woodside, Aberdeen. After their honeymoon the couple settled at 13 Alva Street, Edinburgh, where Dr Bruce took up practice. Theirs was a most congenial union, and thirty years later, Sir Robert Philip, who wrote Bruce's obituary notice, commented:

> In his home he was very happy. An Aberdonian in Edinburgh he returned to Aberdeen for his bride. It seems but a year or two since the Silver Wedding came round, and at his table, to a small party of particular friends, he told of twenty-five years of continual happiness and how he owed them to his wife.

In the first twelve years seven children were born to them. The oldest son, Alexander Ninian, studied medicine, and like his father, specialised in neurology. The second son, James Milne, died when a boy of nine, a sore heart for his parents. The third son, Vincent Connell, an especially lovable boy (we are told) eventually inherited Inverquhomery, but was killed in the Kaiser's War. The fourth son, Walter Marshall, who carried on the family tradition in shipping, became the last Bruce Laird of Inverquhomery. Of the daughters, the eldest, Annie Louisa, married in 1913 Dr S A Kinnier Wilson, of Harley Street, London. Mary, the second daughter was born and died on the same day, 18 June 1891. The youngest daughter, Hilda Gertrude, born 13 March 1893, married in 1914 Mr George Martin Gray, a founder member of Gray and Gray, solicitors, Peterhead.

In 1899, after all their children had been born to them, and perhaps for more elbow room, Dr and Mrs Bruce removed to 8 Ainslie Place, Edinburgh, from where he continued his practice. Their new home became more and more an abode of domestic felicity and hospitable entertainment. His wife's capability and good management relieved him of any anxiety regarding the children or household affairs, and she gave him encouragement in running his practice on the family doctor image rather than as a business concern. Nevertheless, in those early days, when he was struggling to make a name for himself, life was an uphill pull, for his toil elicited but a scant return. 'In his early career', writes Sir Leslie MacKenzie, 'he must have had many a hard day. He told me once how the consultants of his junior days would ask him out to do any post-mortem examinations, complimented him ''on the extraordinary enthusiasm of you scientific fellows'', but they never offered him a fee! They conveniently forgot that he had to live as well as to think. But there was no bitterness in Bruce's composition. His kindliness broke through and modified his whole life.' People may have taken advantage of his obliging nature, yet it was this quality of mind that enabled him to make headway. People saw the depth and valued the modesty of the young practitioner and he quickly emerged from general practice and plunged with characteristic thoroughness into pathological and neurological research.

But his friends were never neglected and 'Number Eight' became a sort of guest house for all who were sincere in their concern for the advancement of neurological science. These sometimes included distinguished physicians from abroad, but all were sure of a hearty welcome and a wholesome meal in the family dining room.

As a general practitioner Bruce worked just as hard as he had done as a student, and what with his hospital and laboratory commitments even moreso, so that his social and recreative pursuits were severely restricted. But if he worked hard he played hard and always seemed to go in at the deep end in any diversion that attracted him. He even found time to play golf, and according to Sir Robert Philip (his obituarist):

> If he worked hard it was not that he could not play, but that he couldn't find the time for it. Years ago, one lovely morning in June, I remember once going with him round the Balgownie golf-course at Aberdeen, redolent with the scent of gorse and thyme, and the tang of the sea, on a perfect summer day. [obviously before the 'pong' from the Don in the sixties and seventies] As he pressed the turf with fondness he remarked 'We should do this once or twice a week'. But alas he never found the time for it.

He did have the occasional 'Hare shoot' with a company of friends in the autumn over the fields at Millhill, and he also enjoyed an outing astride the new 'velocipede' bicycles that were so popular in the late Victorian era.

Even his hobbies can scarcely be said to have afforded much relief from the mental pressure to which he subjected himself in the course of his duties. He loved history and was especially fond of collecting memorabilia on Mary Queen of Scots, perhaps in his quest for Stuart ancestry and the family's supposed descent from King Robert I. Old Edinburgh always appealed to him, where he used to rummage about collecting books and engravings of the city and of old town landmarks and closes as they appeared in former days. The books made quite a feature in his library, as did the engravings, hung round about the walls of his dining room, which gave it quite an old world character. 'He certainly had his "off" days, and when free, no one entered with more zest into his recreation and sport.'

His biographer met him twice at 8 Ainslie Place. He was the Rev Adam Mackay, one-time minister of Cruden Parish Church, author of the *Distinguished Sons Of Cruden*, in which appears a cameo of Alexander Bruce, and to which I am much indebted for background information for my story. The Rev Mackay tells us:

> Socially he was much loved. Though an eager student and by nature something of a recluse, no one knew better the value of good fellowship, or sought more consistently to do his duty as a citizen and friend. He was a member of St Cuthbert's Parish Church, and an intimate companion of its worthy minister, the very Rev Dr Macgregor. On 22 April 1883, he was ordained to the eldership, and few members of that illustrious Kirk Session were more faithful in their office, an appointment he held until his untimely death. As a medical adviser to the Standard Life Assurance Company, and later to The Scottish Widow's Fund, he also mingled freely with the stalwarts of the city and was esteemed by them for breadth of outlook and bonhomie. He was one of the original members of the Pathological Society; and the late Sir Sims Woodhead tells us that at the annual meetings, after the strenuous labours of the day (to which he contributed valuable material and suggestion) he 'was always in great form at the dinner—his geniality, shrewdness and humorous stories were ever welcome'. In his home he was an ideal husband, father and host. His home was his sanctuary, and no rough voice of the world ever intruded there, 'His private life', writes Sir Robert Philip, was simple, quiet and cheerful. His qualities of heart were no less esteemed than his qualities of head. A numerous band of friends were deeply attached to him. He enjoyed the social board with congenial company. Whether as host or guest, he made things go brightly. How wonderfully the interesting face with its reserve, bordering on solemnity, would light up with a smile or with the play of humour. He enjoyed a good story, and told one well, his serious features and language

only adding zest to the tale.' With one friend, or student who had won his confidence, he was at his best. Then he threw aside all reserve, and out of the rich stores of his mind and heart gave forth his treasures freely. It was my privilege to meet him but once or twice. On one of these occasions he invited me to come and see him in Edinburgh. I called in the morning and was shown into his consulting room—a beautiful, bright room, handsomely furnished as a library, and fitted with the latest electrical appliances, etc., for the treatment of nervous troubles. 'Come and dine with me at 7 o'clock,' he said, 'I will be free them.' I went, and spent a very happy and educative evening. After dinner he took me up to his 'den'. I found it was his real workshop—a room similar in size to his consulting room, with an even bigger library. One had to steer a pathway, however, over a carpet covered with manuscripts and books with which he was working; though these, I noticed, were carefully and even neatly arranged. 'Now we will be comfortable', he said; and having drawn up our chairs to the fire, he proceeded to 'pour wisdom' into me—frank expressions of opinion about men and manners, a minister's work, and the work on which he himself was engaged. I was impressed among other things by his regard for the late Dr Macgregor (he was indeed enthusiastic in his praise) and by a remark which he made regarding the possibility of establishing communication with the spirit world. 'Only the foolish', he said, 'will dare to dogmatise'. On another of these occasions he did me the kindness of opening our annual Sale of Work in connection with Cruden Parish Church, and all were impressed by his earnest plea for increased support of the Church's Medical Mission. That was in 1910, when his health was beginning to show signs of uncertainty. A remark which he made to me afterwards in the manse garden has, looking back upon it, a pathetic significance. 'Keep out of the city', he said, 'as long as you honestly can. When you are on the wheel you have got to go round; and sometimes its grind is merciless.'

By 1883 Bruce had firmly established himself in his chosen profession. He also began to write up those vast stores of knowledge which were to fit him for the work of a specialist. He took classes on Histology and Pathology of the nervous system at Surgeon's Hall, lectures which were eagerly attended and he excelled as a teacher. Knowing his subject thoroughly he was never at a loss, and his sense of quiet power impressed his students. They knew that they were absorbing proved data which would serve them well in future experience and they gave him studied attention. But there was no display or ostentation in his methods; no evidence of authority or superior knowledge, though a quiet gleam of humour now and then relieved the gravity of his discourses. 'Whether at the bedside, in the laboratory or in the classroom', wrote a fellow-student, 'Bruce was an ideal teacher. Sound in method and principles, sure of his facts, clear, concise, and deliberate in exposition, he convinced his students at the point of demonstration and argument . . . one felt that he was a teacher, not born indeed, but trained in the best school of accurate method and of unbounded, if restrained, enthusiasm.'

In research also he was likewise painstaking and persevering. In the words of one of his pupils he

> . . . never ceased to think anatomically. Thus, for example, impressed by the peculiar features of the cells of the intermedio-lateral tract in the spinal cord, he saw at once that for an authoritative study the investigation of the whole cord in a series of consecutive sections was imperative; and, undaunted by the magnitude of the task set him by his own imagination, he proceeded to cut a normal cord into no less than some 6,000 serial sections, and counted, not once or twice only, the cells of the tract above named in each section, with the result that finality is stamped indelibly on this magistral contribution to nervous anatomy.

INVERQUHOMERY

Dr Bruce's father had died in 1885 and left his mother a widow at Millhill. How long she remained on the farm is not clearly known, but she survived her husband by fourteen years and died in Aberdeen at the age of sixty-nine in 1899. By all appearances her son did not long associate himself with Millhill, which was to be expected, when he was so fully involved in medical science. Millhill was on the Kinmundy Estate, owned by one of the Fergusons of Pitfour, and when the Fergusons relinquished their estates around 1925, it may be assumed that Millhill was also sold, probably to Mr Fowlie of Aberdour Home Farm, whose son would have been the leasee of Millhill at the time, and during the present composition in 1985 a member of the Fowlie family still farms at Millhill.

In 1900, a year after the death of Dr Bruce's mother (Mary Milne) James Bruce Esquire, the resident Laird of Inverquhomery also died. As James Bruce had no family he had directed his trustees that on the death of his wife, Mrs Diana Bruce, née Wheeler, which occurred on 10 April 1904, they convey his estate to his grand nephew, Vincent Connell Bruce. Vincent Connell was the third son of Dr Bruce, and still a minor in his sixteenth year. Everyone expected that the estate would be left to Dr Bruce himself; but some misgivings on the part of his uncle decided him to direct it to Dr Bruce's third son.

The late Laird may have considered that for the little interest that his nephew took in Millhill (being so much preoccupied with medical science) he was better left out of it, and went over his head to his third son, who was not yet settled in life, and a most intelligent and likeable lad, according to all reports. It could also be said that by conceding his estate to Vincent Bruce the Laird had also subordinated the elder brother Ninian, probably for the same reason that he had excluded the father—that Ninian was also by then taking up medicine as a career. John, the second son, you may remember, had died at the age of nine.

The old Laird seems to have been a man of somewhat eccentric habit and unpredictable action, determined on keeping everybody in their place on the social scale and on their toes at his command. His temper was especially trying on tenantry and servants, and at his funeral, after the gravedigger had filled in the grave, he smoothed it over with the back of his spade and was heard to mutter: 'Aye, aye, Laird, that's the hinmost job I'll dae for ye. Aye; and it's the only wan ye havna found faut wi'.'

Strictly speaking there were two estates, Inverquhomery and Longside. They had been bought by Dr Bruce's grand-uncle, the first James Bruce (1787–1862) at different times, but the mansion house being on the estate of Inverquhomery, the proprietor of both estates came to be spoken of as 'the Laird of Inverquhomery'. In my own time the Laird of Inverquhomery was the only resident laird left in the parish and he was known simply as 'the Lairdie'. All the Lairds and their ladies are interred in the Inverquhomery burial ground and have their plaques on the roofless walls of the ruined kirk just inside the Lych-Gate of the old graveyard at Longside. On the other side of the newer church Jamie Fleeman and the Rev John Skinner of 'Tullochgorum' fame sleep with them into eternity. The first Bruce Laird was a personal friend of the Rev Skinner, and when he died the poet wrote a lengthy epitaph which may still be read on his tombstone.

> Here lies confined a while to promised rest,
> In hopes to rise again among the Blest,
> The precious dust of one whose course of life
> Knew neither fraud, hypocrisy, nor strife;
> A husband loving, and of gentle mind,
> A father careful, provident, and kind,
> A farmer, active with no greedy view,
> A Christian pious, regular, and true,
> One who in quiet trod the private stage
> Of rural labour to a ripe old age:
> Beloved by neighbours, honoured by his own,
> Lived without spot and dy'd without a groan,
> Long may his humble virtues be rever'd,
> Long be his name remembered with regard.
> And long may Agriculture's School produce
> Such honest men as Alexander Bruce.

Vincent Bruce, 'wise beyond his years', referred at his coming-of-age celebration, to this 'apple of discord which had been thrown into the midst of the family', and boldly spoke of his grand-uncle's will as 'terribly vexing and disappointing'. 'It would have exasperated most men', he said, 'and soured many. My father however, although overlooked, has never shown the slightest irritation. It has only served to draw us closer together.' Referring to Ninian his brother he stated that 'although he is my elder brother, and has also been deprived of his proper position in relation to the estate, I am happy to say that fact has never made any difference between us. Ninian is endowed with mental ability, and is already on the way to a successful career. One would almost think', he added modestly, 'that the late Mr Bruce had a shrewd idea of our respective abilities'.

The estate, charmingly situated, extends to 1,500 acres, and comprises, in addition to the mansion house, a large Home Farm, thirteen tenant farms, and a great part of the village of Longside, although this latter property has subsequently been sold. The farms contain some of the richest soil in Aberdeenshire but are no longer included in the estate. In Dr Bruce's time however the lands were intact, and looking after the property for his son provided him with a new incentive, as if he didn't have enough on his plate already. Perhaps the situation was more congenial to his taste and circumstances than had been the case fifteen years earlier at Millhill when his own father died, especially now that he had achieved much of his ambition in neurology, though his chores in medicine were by no means complete. And of course he would not be perennially responsible for the estate; it was but an interim period until his son could take over the management, and his son's future prospects was his main concern. Vincent was only a lad of sixteen and perhaps his father felt it was but another line of duty to give him all the assistance he could muster, assisted by some advice from factor or overseer. Now he devoted much of his leisure in the summer months to the administration of the estate. He was now fifty and maybe he felt he could seek his roots again in the cornlands of Buchan. Inverquhomery became a sort of 'Balmoral' for the family, and they went north from Edinburgh each year for their holidays. In his walks along the beech avenues and on his journeys to Longside the worthy Doctor came to be identified, as were his ancestors, as 'the Laird'.

He tried to be the good proprietor, now keenly interested in all matters relating to agriculture, and deeply concerned for the welfare of his tenants and cottar servants. He wanted them to have the best in living conditions and housing that the estate could afford them. In 1908 he was elected President of the Buchan Club, and it was a happy day for him when he entertained the members at the mansion house, where he delivered his presidential address on 'The Last Earl Marischal', an historic memoir on the Keith family of Inverugie, which can still be read in section 10 of Tocher's *Book of Buchan* for 1910, published by the Buchan Field Club.

CELEBRATION

An even happier event for Dr Bruce was the celebration to mark the twenty-first birthday of his son Vincent, when he became fully responsible for the management of the estate. This occurred on 20 April 1909, a day on which the village and neighbourhood

of Longside was in holiday mood, the village gay with flags and
bunting and banners and streamers across the main street and
up the Inn Brae. A large gathering of tenants and friends
assembled to honour the young heir and his father and mother
at Inverquhomery House, and where possible the servants
shared in the festivities. John Ross Imray, the resident poet of
the period, composed a poem in honour of the event, of which
I will give here three of the verses to illustrate the general whole-
heartedness of the occasion, and the popularity of the Bruce
Lairds among the residents.

> Blithe Buchan cronies, far an' near,
> On Ugie's wimplin' tide,
> Mair sae on Inverquhomery's lan's
> An' village o' Longside!
> Come ane, come a', baith great and sma',
> Frae youth tae auld grey beard,
> An' welcome to his heritage
> Oor bricht young laird!
>
> Let buntin' wave upon the breeze
> This blithesome April day;
> Let bonfire bleeze at mirken 'oor
> Upon the 'Yellow Brae'!
> An' while we watch the flarin' pile,
> May cheer on cheer be heard
> Frae lips and he'rts, love bumper fu',
> For oor youg laird!
>
> Descendant o' an honoured race,
> Wha've lang by us been kent,
> Aneth whase kind, judicious sway
> We liv'd in sweet content;
> Sae, like his predecessors gane,
> Lang, lang may he be spared
> Tae be a counsellor and frien',
> As oor gweed laird!

Alas John Imray's wish and prayer were not granted, but we
shall come to that later. Meanwhile a dinner was afterwards
arranged in St John's Hall in the village 'Crescent', facing the
policies of Cairngall, a rival estate whose friendly owner, Major
James Hutchinson no doubt attended the banquet. The local

doctor presided over 100 guests and addressed them with a glowing tribute for the young laird and his father. Vincent returned his thanks:

> I could not help thinking that the warmth of the reception given me today is largely due to the fact that I am the son of my father. He is a Buchan man born and bred; his heart has always been in Buchan. More and more I feel the strength and help and inspiring influence of my father. During my years of adolescence and apprenticeship my father has borne upon his shoulders the burden of looking after my interests and those of the tenants on the estate; and has given to them of his time, care and thought ungrudgingly.

Dr Bruce, acknowledging the toast and success of the gathering concluded with the promise that, 'whatever could be done for the good of the estate, the tenants and feuars, will be done by me and my boy.'

It has been remarked upon, in the words of Sir Leslie MacKenzie, that the secret of Dr Bruce's happiness and charm on these occasions was his affection for Buchan and its people.

> He was an Aberdonian through every fibre of his nature. He loved the life of the farm, the ripening crops and the thriving cattle and the greenery of wood and pasture—the life that gave him his fine career. To that he went back as to an unfailing friend. Like Faust he had the deep conviction that all our knowledge and our experience, and our infinitely rich adventure of life, have this for their true end—to redeem a waste land from the sea and make the life of our fellow-men more warm and happy.

HIS FINAL LABOURS

Dr Bruce returned to Edinburgh refreshed and heartened from his sojourn in Buchan, but heavily overburdened with a backlog of work and time consuming commitments. Besides his consulting practice, his hospital and laboratory work demanded his attention, and several books and papers on neurology he had written or translated required to be edited and proofed for publication. Some of these works were immeasurably valuable for their period, and useful for student and layman in simplifying the complications of 'Desseminated Sclerosis', 'The Lymphatics of the Spinal Cord', 'Multiple Neuromata of the Central Nervous System, their structure and Histogenesis'.

He had as co-worker at this time Dr James W Dawson, 'one of the most brilliant neurological histologists in the country'; and Dr Dawson tells us that Bruce's scientific zeal was such that to be associated with him was in itself a sufficient reward.

> For there were times when those who worked under him in the laboratory seemed to share with him, and have their enthusiasm kindled by, the clear view which he possessed of fundamental and ultimate truths. They then recognised how he had long before seen the far-reaching significance of the smallest detail, and had patiently related all the details to one another and brought them to focus. He hailed with greatest delight each new observation that seemed to realise his premonitions. We felt that we had been in contact with a man whose work had let in a ray of light into a dark place.

Dr Bruce's labours on behalf of neurological science multiplied rather than diminished towards the end of his life, and where work was concerned he refused to spare himself. In the words of one of his compeers:

> Dr Bruce was a strenuous worker, and it was only by a systematic economy of his time that he was able to keep abreast of his multifarious duties. More than once after talks with him, I felt that he was encroaching too much on his physical reserves. He never relaxed the pressure of his student days, and none but his fellow students could know what that meant. Work was his passion. When old Edinburgh men forgathered, and the familiar question 'How goes Edinburgh?' had been passed round, another question commonly asked was, 'and Bruce as hard at it as ever?' It was he largely who gave to Edinburgh her distinctive place in neurology. He was one of the men enquired about by strangers who knew Edinburgh from the distance. A friend once told me that he dared to reproach Bruce for doing too much and warned him that he might prematurely end his life. 'I know the risks too well', was the quiet answer, 'but sometimes it is a duty to take these risks.'

In the consulting room he was equally painstaking. The serious approach and quiet manner, sometimes lost on unruly students, was more appreciated by patients who were seriously ill, and who knew the professional from the quack, the gold from the dross. Thy knew that what was uppermost in his mind was their malady and cure, and that what was humanly possible would be done for them. Dr J H Harvey Pirie, a native of Ellon, Aberdeenshire, who was assistant to Dr Bruce at the time of his death, wrote: 'To his patients, both private and in hospital, he was ever the beloved physician. His services were much in demand, and to all he gave his best ungrudingly.'

In October 1890, Dr Bruce was appointed Fifth Assistant Physician in the Royal Infirmary, Edinburgh, the first of a series of appointments which culminated in his becoming Third Ordinary Physician four years before his death. Both as teacher and consultant he was eminently fitted for these appointments. According to Sir Robert Philip:

> He brought to the problems of the bedside an uncommon store of exact knowledge—physiological and pathological . . . Accuracy of clinical observation he demanded from his students as he demanded from himself. Often he would lament the declension of self-training in the clinical wards of the Infirmary. He yearned to see men soak themselves in clinical material.

Evidently he spared no pains to secure the best results, for his patients and for his students. Each forenoon he attended the Infirmary and went the rounds of his wards. The students gathered to his side as he went quietly from bed to bed, thoroughly and considerately, while he noted the requirements of his patients and prescribed for them, informing his students and asking their opinions on individual cases. 'A walk round with Bruce' was considered an education in itself, both as regards method and practicality. He was also a pioneer in the demand for Psychiatric Wards for the treatment of the 'insipient and transient cases of insanity', which is now accepted practice.

Sir Leslie MacKenzie reports on one particular case where the symptoms had baffled several doctors. Bruce made a careful examination of the patient and gave his opinion that the trouble was caused by a haemorrhage in a certain group of fibres in the spinal cord near the ninth or tenth dorsal vertebrae. His diagnosis was correct, as proved later under microscopic observation. When the spot was observed where the mischief centered, Bruce became very excited and a delighted 'Ah!' escaped him. Exactly what he had foretold had been verified for all to see.

In 1909 the University of Aberdeen conferred on him the degree of LLD. No greater compliment could have been accorded to a scientific worker than that paid him by the Dean of Faculty of Law in presenting him for his degree. 'His works and writings in the department of neurology are known wherever neurology is studied, and in some respects may be regarded as epoch-making. It is not too much to say that there is no neurologist in Britain whose work has better stood the test of time.'

EXHAUSTION AND DEATH

Dr Bruce held fourteen appointments in the Royal Infirmary of Edinburgh, wrote or translated five books, and with others con-tributed forty-five papers on neurology and its diseases. In August 1910, he finished his translation of Oppenheim's 'Text-Book of Nervous Diseases', and went off for a two months' holiday. But the following winter his health gave way. By December he showed unmistakable signs of nervous disorder and exhaustion. He became a victim of the neurosis he had studied for a lifetime; a martyr to his own scholarship, and he was in-voluntarily prostrated at the feet of the idol he had created but could not control. In searching for a cure for others he had killed himself. In March of 1911 he went south to rest at Bournemouth, Dawlish and Torquay. But to no avail, and he returned to Edinburgh at the end of April resigned to his fate. Depression and decline consumed him though he bore the affliction without complaint. Perhaps he had reached a stage when he didn't realise even himself what ailed him. Mercifully he passed away peace-fully at home on 4 June 1911.

By his own desire he was buried at Longside. 'On Thursday 8 June', writes one who was present, 'Edinburgh restored to Buchan the mortal remains of her adopted son, crowned with laurels.' The previous day there had been a service in Edinburgh, in St Cuthbert's Parish Church, where Dr Bruce had been an elder, and the ceremony was conducted by the two collegiate ministers of that charge, the Rev George G D S Duncan and the

Rev W Lyall Wilson. In attendance were representatives of
Edinburgh Royal Infirmary, the Royal College of Physicians,
and the University of Edinburgh.

The following day (8 June) while the whole neighbourhood
mourned, Dr Bruce was laid to rest at Longside, where every
window-blind was down, and over Inverquhomery House the
flag was at half-mast. Besides the members of his family who had
travelled north for the interment were members of the Royal
College of Physicians, including the President, Dr Bryan
Bramwell, accompanied by others and including Sir Robert
Philip, Dr Pirie, Professor Muir of Glasgow and many others.
They were met at Longside station by representatives of the
University of Aberdeen, including six members of the deceased's
old arts class, and friends representative of almost every public
institution in the north. The cortege was followed into the village
by a very large crowd of mourners and school children who had
assembled to pay a last tribute of respect to one who had brought
honour and fame to the neighbourhood. The service in the Parish
Church was conducted by the Rev Richard Henderson (Old
Dick) and he was ably assisted by the Rev R Mackay, minister
of the Episcopal Church of St John. The principal hymn was
'Now the Labourer's Task is O'er', and after the benediction the
coffin was carried across the sward to the ruined church of 1620,
followed by his three sons, and solemnly interred in the family
burial ground.

The premature death of the doctor deeply distressed Mrs
Bruce and laid a burden of sorrow on the family, a sadness that
was shared by their many friends and by medical science world
wide. What might have been is mindless speculation, yet in all
probability, had Bruce lived another ten years he would have
been rewarded with recognition and honour for his noble endeavour in the realms of medical science. In the words of his
biographer:

> For Bruce himself, doubtless, the next dozen years would have
> meant recognition long overdue; and a series of appointments
> worthy of his achievements—who knows? What one cannot help
> regretting is that a life, so nobly inclined and so eminently endowed,
> should have been cut short at the zenith of its strength and powers,
> and when it seemed fully equipped to help and bless the world.

But even that regret is transistory. For Bruce's real work was done in the obscure period of early life when he made himself master of his subject, and in those lonely hours of toil when he grouped together the results of his knowledge and gave them to the world.

VINCENT CONNELL BRUCE

Yet there is another side to the picture, the darker side of the mirror that Bruce was spared the sight of, though his wife and remaining family bore it bravely. Just three years after the Doctor's death the Great War of 1914–18 began, and his son Vincent Connell joined up as a private in the 15th Royal Scots Regiment. Shortly afterwards he received a Commission in the 13th Royal Scots, but he applied for a transference to the 5th Battalion of the Gordon Highlanders, the regiment of Longside and the county, and in December of 1914 his application was granted.

Vincent had been studying Law in Edinburgh and graduated LLB in 1913. Only six months before his enlistment he had been called to the Scottish Bar, and his future prospects seemed bright and secure. In 1900, when it became known that he was to inherit Inverquhomery his father sent him to Oxford, where he graduated BA in 1909 with first class honours in history. On 1 May 1915, he crossed the Channel with his battalion for France. In March 1916, the 5th Gordons were holding the region of Neuville St Vaast, when the Germans exploded a mine beneath a section of the line where Lieutenant Bruce was visiting his men. No trace of him could be found. 'I fear', wrote General Douglas Campbell, to his mother, 'that there is no longer room for any doubt as to the fate of your gallant son—he was buried in the mine which the Germans exploded in the trenches held by the 5th Gordon Highlanders on the night of the 25–26 March . . . Your son was a very brave officer . . . If any dangerous work had to be done, he was always ready to volunteer. He was also a most conscientious and hard working officer, and whatever he took up he gave all his energies to it . . . His death is a great loss, not only to his battalion, but to the army.' 'Our noblest and best loved officer,' wrote Major S McDonald, 'everyone loved him— men and officers alike.' Seven years earlier the village folk of

Longside rejoiced with their young Laird on his twenty-first birthday—and now they mourned his passing. A memorial tablet of white Sicilian marble is embedded in the west gable of the old church at Longside. It is all that remains of Vincent Connell Bruce.

CONCLUSION

Annie Louisa Connell, wife of Doctor Bruce, died at Inverquhomery on 2 June 1923, seven years after her son, and the estate was ceded to her youngest son, Walter Marshall Bruce, probably in deference to his surviving elder brother, Dr Alexander Ninian Bruce, who, like his father, was fully preoccupied in medical science and may have declined hereditary rights, the second time this had happened to him. He was the oldest son, and like his brothers was educated at George Watson's College. He studied at Edinburgh University, where he graduated MD and DSc, specialising like his father in the Science of Neurology. He succeeded as editor of the *Review of Neurology and Psychiatry*, the periodical his father had founded and edited some six years before he died. Ninian also served with distinction in the Great War, specialising on nervous disorders and shell-shock, and was demobolised with the rank of Lieut-Colonel in the RAMC. He returned to his practice in Edinburgh, and also as lecturer on Neurology at the University. He died in ripe years age eighty-six in 1968, having been predeceased by his wife, Louisa Hogarth, who died in 1949.

Completing his education at Merchiston Castle, Edinburgh, Walter Marshall Bruce chose the career of his grand-uncle, James Bruce Esquire, of Inverquhomery and entered a shipping office and went out to East Africa. During the First World War he returned to take part in the struggle, which meant three brothers in uniform. He became an officer in the 6th Gordon Highlanders. In 1917 he was severely wounded at Albert, and on recovery was transferred to the East African Rifles, where his knowledge of the native language proved invaluable. On being demobilised, he returned to his shipping interests and was for a period stationed in Zanzibar and at Mombasa.

In 1923 Walter Marshall married Janet Ruth Walker, daughter
of Dr James Walker, who for some time held a Government post
in Borneo, in the East Indies, where Janet was born in 1892. Dr
Walker had the distinction of being the first white doctor in
Borneo. In 1899 he returned to England and took up practice at
Chudley in South Devon. At ninety-three years of age Mrs Janet
Bruce (née Walker) is a sprightly old lady who still gets about on
her stick and welcomes her visitors with a firm and friendly
hand clasp. Her white, wrinkled features belie the youthful
radiance of her peat brown eyes, and she still conveys an image
of elegance and good breeding in her stalwart frame. She is the
oldest human being I have ever talked with, and in her cultivated
manner of speech one becomes aware of a genuine specimen of
the 'to the manor born' genus, and as she faced me in her armchair she was the picture of the Laird's wife as I had imagined
her. Formerly a talented artist some of her paintings adorn the
walls of her ornately furnished home. She asked if any of my
family were writers and I told her I had a granddaughter who
wrote poems. Raising her staff she pointed to one of her paintings, then at one on the sideboard by one of her granddaughters
and remarked: 'It misses a generation you know!' and there was
the authority of age and wisdom in her statement.

She told me that Walter Marshall had proposed to her in the
conservatory at Inverquhomery, while she was there on holiday.
'He was with the P & O Line at that time you know,' she empha-
sised, 'under Lord Inchcape, and I remember him telling me that
when he first went there for an interview Inchcape said to him:
''If you never do more than you're paid for you'll never be paid
for more than you do!''—and my husband never forgot it and
worked very hard for the Company.' She said she felt that she
had found her roots at Inverquhomery, because James Cheves,
who was her grandfather, had once been the banker at Longside.
When her husband retired from shipping they moved north from
Edinburgh and took up permanent residence at Inverquhomery.
This was in 1923 and three daughters were born to them. Moyra
Beatrice Connell Bruce was born in Edinburgh, the others at
Inverquhomery.

Moyra devoted her life to nursing and never married and now
looks after her mother in the family mansion house in Queen's
Road, Aberdeen, where the Bruces took up residence when they

left Inverquhomery in 1955. The second daughter, Doreen Mary Bruce, studied Physiotherapy at Edinburgh University. She married Mr Alexander Mitchell, managing director of Paton's Travel Services. They have a son and daughter and live at Bieldside, on the western outskirts of Aberdeen. The youngest daughter, Audrey Marshall Bruce, married London business man Mr John Quiggin; they have two daughters and live at Wimbledon in London. The Bruce girls were educated at home, privately, and Audrey, the youngest daughter also went to University. But Moyra still has memories of all the farms and their tenants on the estate, and she remembers cycling to T S Davidson's Post Office Emporium in Longside for the *Scotsman* newspaper for her father. She also remembers walking to church, where her father was an Elder, and used to go round the pews with a long-handled wooden ladle to take the collection. They did have a car, a Crossley, and both parents could drive, though mostly to the village for provisions and seldom for pleasure. Her father, Moyra said, had been a member of almost every Committee associated with the welfare of the Parish and County, and that he overworked himself in Public Service, to which he was devoted and sincere. The daughters are the last of the Bruces of Inverquhomery; the final chapter in nearly 300 years of family history.

When Walter Bruce took up residence at Inverquhomery the farm was severely run down from its former reputable position in agriculture. Of the famous pedigree herd of Shorthorns only two cows remained, and this to supply milk for the family of the resident gardener, who was all that remained of the former staff. In the six years since the death of Vincent Bruce there had been no resident Laird, and the affairs of the estate had been looked after by a visiting factor. Walter Marshall had to start from scratch to restock the farm. Cultivation and grazing had also been sadly neglected, with thistles, dockens and tanzies taking possession of the fields. Fencing and drainage had also been forgotten and the soil had to be reinvigorated with the plough and manure to bring it back to fertility. In thirty-two years, however, the last Bruce Laird brought the Home Farm back to the flourishing tradition of his ancestors, and but for a heart attack in 1946 he might have held the fort for some more years. Without a male heir however, and tempted by a lucrative offer from James

Donald of Portlethen, on behalf of Sainsbury Ltd, the meat and chain-store conglomeration, he sold the estate and moved into Aberdeen. Sainsbury's intention was (and probably still is) to utilise Inverquhomery as a sort of live meat safe in reserve over lean periods, like January after the Christmas sales and May–June before the flush of the grazing season, balanced in rotation of course with the customary root and cereal crops. Only one tenant remains on the estate; the others bought their holdings or have been taken over by Sainsburys, and all the property in Longside village has been disposed of.

Walter Bruce enjoyed six years of retirement in Aberdeen and died in 1961 at the age of seventy-one. During the Second World War, while resident at Inverquhomery, he was my commanding officer in the Home Guard at Longside. As Major Bruce he awarded me with a stripe and made me a lance-corporal, which was the peak of my achievement in the armed forces. He was very kind to me, and on being informed by a brother officer that I had recently recovered from severe pneumonia he exempted me from crawling through fields of wet grass on manoeuvres. He put a feather in my cap when he told me that if ever he wanted anyone for map-reading, or for strategic reconnaissance, I would be the one he would light upon. He even took an interest in the books I read, and complimented on my perusal of *The Forsyte Saga*, by John Galsworthy, probably because I was the only one in the platoon who would attempt it. Nor could he have guessed that such eccentric reading in a farm worker would lead to my writing a potted biography of his father.

Even today, forty years on, I remember Major Bruce with a pleasant flicker of pride; moreso when I watch a repeat of 'Dad's Army' on television, for he was the non-spitting image of the late Arthur Lowe in battledress. The physical resemblance is remarkably similar: roundish face and slight moustache, rather forced smile in awkward circumstances, almost grudgingly acquiescent; the bluff, stocky figure with the cane-under-arm, dammit lads, stand firm attitude that made him for me the standard prototype of Arthur Lowe. But of course he would never have allowed himself to be badgered into the ridiculous situations of 'Dad's Army' repute, not even when Geordie Crisp dropped a hand-grenade from which he had pulled the priming pin, though he did run like the rest of us to get clear of the explosion. And if a crofter recruit had a mare at the foaling, a 'coo at the calvin' or 'a soo at the farrowin'', leave of absence was readily granted, for the Major Laird was in a position to know the pressures and anxieties of their lives and took the risk of being out of favour with General Sir John Burnett-Stewart of Crichie House, who was Commander in Chief of HM Forces in the County. But physically at least Major Bruce was Arthur Lowe, and the family agree with my opinion and also with my respect for his memory as 'The Lairdie'.

RAFAEL CARLOS GORDON

Some years before his death, General Franco of Spain appointed the present Juan Carlos as his successor and legitimate heir to the Spanish throne. But it is the present king's grandparents, King Alfonso XIII of Spain, and his queen, Victoria Eugenia, who concern us here, when they spent part of their honeymoon at Wardhouse, at the back o' Bennachie, when Rafael Gordon was laird.

Princess Victoria Eugenia, 'Ena', was the daughter of Queen Victoria's youngest daughter, Princess Beatrice. Her father was Henry, Prince of Battenberg, whom Queen Victoria referred to as 'Liko', her 'ray of light', and whose masculine presence consoled her immeasureably in old age, like a reflected image of her dear departed Albert. Prince Henry died at sea of malaria in 1896, returning from the Ashanti Expendition to the Gold Coast, so he never saw his daughter married.

Like our own Princess Anne, Eugenia was a keen horsewoman and at seven years of age was 'tossed and rolled upon by her pony', causing great concern to her ageing grandmother, who was afraid of brain damage. But all was well, and Eugenia grew up 'a lovely fair-haired Princess who took on the hazardous duty as Queen of Spain.'

King Alfonso (1886–1941) acceded to the Spanish throne in May 1886 and was deposed on 14 April 1931 by the Fascists of General Franco's regime. The king would have been twenty years old and his queen nineteen when they were at Wardhouse, and a journalist of the period wrote of her as 'so fair and placid, and majestic, such a solemn contrast to her boyish, nervous looking, energetic husband . . .' But Alfonso has been referred to as a good king who did much for the Spanish people and got little thanks for it, and at his going perhaps they 'never missed the watter or the wallie ran dry'. He had been King of Spain from the day of his birth, a boy wonder in his day.

During their stay in August, 1906, the Royal couple also visited Fyvie Castle, where they stayed for four days, 13 to 17 August, and we have a wee poem by local poet James Gower to celebrate the occasion, 'Lines on the visit of the King and Queen of Spain to Fyvie Castle':

> Welcome, welcome, illustrious Strangers,
>   To Fyvie's sweet belov'd domain
> Rest thou in peaceful leisure,
>   From the cares of state in sunny Spain.
>
> Glad are we, illustrious Strangers,
>   That both are spared from Assassin's blow
> O'er shaggy heath be thou a ranger,
>   On bank nor braes there lurks no foe.

The 'assassin's blow' concerns the attempt on the lives of the Royal couple in Madrid on their wedding day. Edgar Wallace, novelist of the nineteen-thirties, was an eye-witness to the incident and gave an account of it in the *Daily Mail*, the paper which employed him at the time as a foreign correspondent. He was watching the wedding procession in the Calle Mayor in Madrid and wrote:

> Something made me look up. The windows above both sides of the street were crowded, and, as I raised my eyes, I saw a bunch of flowers hurtling down from an upper window and caught a glimpse of a man's bare hand. The moment I saw those flowers, my heart nearly stopped beating. They were dropping at such a rate that there could be no question that they concealed something heavy, something sinister . . . The force of the explosion almost lifted me off my feet, and in a second I was in the middle of a confused, screaming throng of people, mad with fear. I had a glimpse of dying horses, of blood on the roadway, of a half-fainting queen

being assisted from the carriage, her white dress splashed with blood. But more vivid still is the impression of the king, as he stood up, an immovable smile on his long face, his fingers waving encouragement to the crowd . . .'

Such a consolation then for the Royal newlyweds when they eventually arrived safely in Scotland. Queen Victoria never lived to see her favourite grand-daughter as Queen of Spain, but likewise she was spared the anxiety of this latest outrage, which could have been so much more serious than falling from her pony. Eugenia was a cousin to Kaiser Wilhelm of Germany and niece of the Tzarina of Russia, whose lives had a more tragic effect on history than the fate of the gentle Eurgenia.

They arrived at Wardhouse by carriage and four, in the traditional style of the Gordons of Wardhouse and Kildrummy, who had always been great horsemen, particularly Pedro Carlos Gordon (1806–57) known as the Mad Laird, who drove the mail coach in record time from London to York, and is alleged to have driven his four-in-hand full gallop into Castlehill barracks in Aberdeen. And when the railway came to Keith and Huntly he tried to race the train from Wardhouse to Insch station. But let us hope our young Spanish visitors were driven at a more leisurely pace, affording them time to enjoy the scenery, for the road through Oyne and Insch (where Gadie rins) to Kennethmont is lovely at all times, with the vitrified fort of Dunnideer like a giant's stool on a conical hill overlooking the Shevock burn. They were just a bit early to see Wardhouse in its autumn glory, when the red sunset hangs like the cloak of a matador on the wooded hills, glistening on the rowans and the hips and haws of the dog-rose; when the bracken is a carpet of russet gold, the tinkle of the burns like wine uncorked for the castaneted dance, the wind like soft hands on the tambourines, or the swish of wide skirts in Spanish courtyards. Nestled deep in the Knockandy hillside Wardhouse now stands naked to the bone, a shattered skeleton staring blindly on a former grandeur, hugging its vaultless rooms where Spanish Royalty have tasted whisky, where you can hear the rustle of Spanish lace in the night wind, and the ghostly sighs of its Royal Lovers.

But in 1906 the mansion house still retained its splendour in Spanish architecture, built in the Palladian style in 1757. The entourage included HRH Prince Arthur of Connaught, His Grace the Duke of Richmond and Gordon, El Marques de Viana, El du Duque de Santo Maure and Lord Leith of Fyvie. No secret honeymoon this. Alfonso shook hands with the head gardener and the gamekeeper, Tom Kennedy, whose son was to become a cabinet minister in Ramsay MacDonald's government.

But it was a grand-nephew of the Mad Laird, Rafael Carlos Gordon (1873–1932) known as the Count de Mirasol, who invited the Spanish Monarch and his bride to spend part of their honeymoon on his estates at Wardhouse, near Kennethmont. The Count de Mirasol referred to himself as 'Equerry' or Master of the Queen's Horse, but it was a famous blend of sherry rather than horsemanship that first associated the Gordons of Wardhouse with Spanish Royalty.

The story of the friendship between the Gordons of Wardhouse and the Kings of Spain goes back to the eighteenth century, when James Gordon, the tenth laird of Beldorney in Glass Haugh, and owner of Kildrummy Castle, acquired Wardhouse through marriage to a daughter of the Duke of Fife, the original owners of the estate.

This branch of the Gordon hierarchy was Roman Catholic, and James Gordon's grandson, Charles Edward Gordon (1754–1832) was to bow before the anti-Catholic legislation of the period, preferring to renounce his faith rather than forfeit Wardhouse to the Crown. Charles opted for the life of a resident laird rather than an exile, and indeed, devoted the last twenty years of his life to improving and beautifying his estate in Aberdeenshire.

His younger brother James had private means, and perhaps fearing that further legislation might one day be passed, confiscating the private fortunes of Catholics who refused to give up the faith, he sought refuge in Catholic Spain, where he bought lands and vines in Andalusia, and laid the foundations of a highly successful business. Gordon's sherry was deemed fit for the Spanish Royal table, and thus the Wardhouse family became the friends of Kings. Later, the Laird of Wardhouse's eldest son, John Gordon (1774–1850), joined his uncle in Jerez and after his uncle's death inherited the sherry business. He married in Spain, and the members of his large family also married Spaniards.

Meanwhile, back in Aberdeenshire, John's father, the resident Laird lived to a great age, and the son was sixty before he inherited Wardhouse. But he remained in Spain and died there, and his eldest son, Pedro Carlos Gordon (1806–57) the Mad Laird, set a pattern for his successors by commuting between Andalusia and Wardhouse. It was in his day that the Home Farm was built, the steading like a huge Spanish arena, with its arch and cupola tower, and four-squared courtyard. The great bull-yard within the arena has survived the ghosts of yesteryear, and because it is a listed building it has escaped the hands of the despoiler, thus preserving the Spanish influence at Wardhouse. The mansion house, might be compared with that other famous Gordon residence, Haddo House, near Tarves, but has been much less fortunate than Haddo and is now a ruin.

For nearly two-hundred years the Spanish inheritance has pervaded the Wardhouse Gordons, colouring their names with Spanish titles and their baronial architecture with an aura of Sabatini's *Blood and Sand* and the bull-ring, even to the last laird, who bore Sabatini's christian name of Raphael. Despite the dereliction of scrub and nettles the cloak and sword of Zoro comes to mind at Wardhouse, and one can almost imagine the famous Z scratched with sword point on the harling of the stolid walls surrounding the bullyard.

In 1975, when I interviewed Mr Alexander Souter, owner of the Home Farm, he showed me the original plans of 1841–43, drawn by one William Findlay, and built in the two years by David Wood. Despite the huge area of courtyard, Mr Souter told me there were only chains for thirty cattle, which suggests specialised breeding of pedigree stock, even bulls for the Spanish arenas, and the plans are meticulously marked with fodder barns and turnip sheds and even 'liquid manure tanks', long before our own day of slatted floors and sludge pits for cattle.

Mr Souter had been allowed to roof the open courtyard to house a greater number of loose cattle, but in true Spanish tradition he remains content to live with his family and workers within the quadrangle—no individual farm house and no cottar houses, something I have never seen anywhere else in Scotland. Mr Souter had lived here since 1931, first on lease but later as proprietor on the death of the last laird. He told me that when the 'Big Hoose' was in its glory the head gardener offered to pay half-a-crown to anyone who found a weed in the grounds; now in an autumn breeze the willowherb and thistledown blow like

eiderdown across the policies. He also informed me that when the
Spanish King and Queen were on honeymoon, and returning
from a ride in the Laird's phaeton, they almost collided with a
woodcart in the drive. Mr Souter was six years old at the time
and had retained a clear memory of these events. He was eighty-
one when I spoke to him and he died at the age of ninety on 14
September 1984, an event which induced me to rewrite this
article. His wife, Mary Ann Robertson, whom Jane and I also
met on that occasion, died some five or six years before her
husband.

The Mad Laird, Pedro Carlos, was succeeded on his death in
1857 by his son Juan Jose Gordon, who had been brought up in
Spain, and who was only twenty when he took up residence as
Laird. He invited his Spanish friends to Wardhouse and built the
bull ring behind the mansion for their entertainment. He im-
ported bulls from Spain and held amateur bull-fights on Sunday
afternoons, making himself the 'speak o' the Geerie'.

Juan Jose had married a sister of the Count de Mirasol, thus
bringing the title for the first time to Wardhouse. But he died
young and left no son. The estate passed to his uncle, a younger
brother of the Mad Laird, and from him to his grandson, Rafael
Carlos Gordon, Count de Mirasol, the last Gordon Laird of
Wardhouse. This Rafael Gordon was born in the Royal Palace
in Madrid. He obtained great favour at the Spanish court and
arranged the honeymoon of Alfonso and his bride on his Scottish
estates of Kildrummy and Wardhouse.

During these years of opulence, the Rafael Gordons—the
Count and Countess de Mirasol—visited Wardhouse every summer when the gardens and policies were in full flower, using the
Mansion as a sort of Balmoral, touring the countryside in a
luxurious 1929 Bentley, now scrapped after many idle years in
the nettleyard. Mr Souter's daughter, Mrs Smith (whom we also
met) had childhood memories of the heyday of Wardhouse in the
Rafael Gordon era, when there were great festivities, and when
Rafael's Countess Maria Rodriquez Casanova, a stoutish lady in
black silk, companion friend of Queen Eugenia, came haughtily
through the Home farmhouse with never a 'by-your-leave', but
using the farm kitchen as a sort of back door to the courtyard.

In 1931, when King Alfonso was dethroned, Rafael Gordon
of Wardhouse kept order in Spain, practically ruling the country,

where the poor of Madrid walked on one side of the street and the rich on the other, where no middle-class existed, and the extremes of riches and poverty was a breeding ground for revolution. A year later, when General Franco's hounds were flushing out the aristocracy, Rafael Gordon was forced to flee the country, shadowed as far as London by Franco's scouts, arriving at Wardhouse a penniless fugitive, his Countess left in Spain, and he never saw her again.

After his last lone flight the Count de Mirasol survived but a few months on his old estate in the shadow of Knockandy Hill. Disillusionment overshadowed him and he travelled north to Nairn, seeking the consolation of an old friend. He died suddenly in 1932, suspected of an overdose. There was some confusion over his interment, and in the absence of the Countess he was buried in the family vault at Wallakirk in Glass Haugh. The plaque of grey marble on the wall of the vault is engraved with a simple cross and the following inscription:

GORDONS OF WARDHOUSE
Queen Of Heaven And Mother Of Our God.
Remember That We Belong To Thee.
Preserve And Defend Us As Thy Property And Possession.
Restored By Rafael Gordon Of Wardhouse, 1913.

Perhaps it is a paradox that just two miles along the road from Wardhouse, at Kennethmont, there is a fine modern distillery, but while illicit distilling of whisky was rife in the area the Gordons of Wardhouse chose to press the sweeter grapes of Spain.

After the death of the Count the Mansion House was let out to shooting parties. During the Second World War it was occupied by the soldiery. Compensation paid for damage by the army, just like all the rents paid by the tenant farmers, went to enrich the Spanish Treasury. By 1950 the House was a ruin, the only habitable room was the gunroom, where the farmers paid their rents. The sale of the estate in the nineteen-fifties also took money off to Spain.

Mr Kenneth MacDonald of Gosforth, Newcastle-on-Tyne, whose grandfather was for many years head gardener at Wardhouse assures us that 'Absentee landlords are not much good to a countryside, and I think the best thing that happened to the estate was the sale of the land to farmers like Alex Souter.' He also informs us that his grandfather's wage as head gardener was ten shillings a week at its peak after forty years service. The new owners left the mansion roofless and the fine trees on the estate were all cut down without replanting.

Perhaps we should rejoice in the restoration of Spanish Royalty, proud in the thought that a Gordon of Wardhouse sat for a moment in time in the Spanish Royal Chair, and that he carried the name of Carlos, that of the legitimate heir to the Spanish throne, and perhaps General Franco chose Juan Carlos out of conscience for his grandparents, who we welcomed within our gates all those years ago.

LAIRDS OF FOVERAN

Prior to the Battle of Barra, in 1307, when Robert the Bruce destroyed the Comyn inheritance, the lands of Foveran had been part of the estates or Fiefdom of the Earls of Buchan. Later, in gratitude for the loyalty of his supporters, Bruce awarded Foveran to the Strabroks, a burgess family of Aberdeen, one of whom, William Strabrok, the first proprietor, was twice Provost of the city.

Thirty years later, in the reign of King David II, the Strabroks, who had estates elsewhere, relinquished the barony of Foveran in favour of William de Turin, or Turing, who had attached himself to his sovereign, and had shared King David's exile at the English court. In requital for his services, he, William de Turin, received a royal charter of Foveran, by 'recognition fra Henry de Strabrok', and thus, in 1359 may be considered the first Turing laird of Foveran.

The Turings, of Norman lineage, had formerly lived in Angus; they reigned in Foveran for the next three centuries, and their name became synonymous with the castle they built overlooking the links and the sand dunes and incorporating the legendary Turing Tower and the 'spring well' of Foveran 'under an arch in the wall', from the Gaelic *Fuaran* meaning 'well of the springs'. This well is still in existence under a slab, bubbling away as it has done since medieval times when it served as the castle's main water supply.

The chivalric and crusading adventures of the Turings are commemorated on a stone slab in Foveran Church, known as the Turin Stone, depicting two of their knights in armour resting on their sword hilts, facing each other, under the family crest, and are thought to be two of its members killed at the Battle of Harlaw. It lay for centuries outside in the churchyard, where extremes of weather and the passage of feet eventually cracked it, though it has not in any way diminished the delicate tracery outlining the figures on the stone.

The church, which is a listed building, was built in 1774 and stands across the road from the lodge and entrance to the present Foveran House, which is now a high class Conference Centre for oil-related industries and business functions. Inside the church is an hour-glass from the days of Queen Anne, when the congregation could time the length of the minister's sermon. There is also a font from pre-Reformation days, fashioned from the pillar of a mullioned window in the former church on the same site. In the present building there is a memorial tablet to Foveran's most famous son, the etcher and painter James McBey, who was born in the blacksmith's house just down the road in 1883. He was the illegitimate son of Ann Gillespie, who is buried in the churchyard, a daughter of the blacksmith of the period, William Gillespie, and his wife Mary (McBey's Granny) who also lie at Foveran. McBey's mother resented his birth and the pity of it was that because of her increasing blindness she could not appreciate her son's art work. She caused him great unhappiness and finally hanged herself at 42 Union Gorove in Aberdeen at the age of forty-four. Another of the church's treasures is a fine sculpture work by John Bacon, considered to be one of his finest specimens. Records go back to 1243, when Foveran Church belonged to the Abbey of Deer, and with all these exhibits of a former age it is frequented by many visitors.

A total of twelve successive Turing lairds held the barony of Foveran, which, through marriage, eventually extended to nearly half the parish, adding to the family legacy. The tenth laird, Sir William Turing, was knighted by King James VI, and in 1613 was succeeded by his eldest son, also William, who died three years later, eight days after his marriage, which incurred the following obituary:

The hope, the honour of a noble race,
Here midst this kindred Turing finds a place;
Death paused so long as love's dalliance pleased—
When love abated, death the victim seized.

His brother John inherited the barony and married Barbara, daughter of one of the Gordons of Gight, but they were without issue. He was a staunch Royalist in the Civil War, loyal to Charles I, who made him a baronet in 1639. But alas John, the unlucky twelfth laird, fought for Charles II at Worcester, where defeat cost him his estates and ultimate ruin for the Turing family.

The Forbeses of Tolquhon were the next lairds of Foveran, and during their possession, in 1720, the Turing Tower collapsed, fulfilling a rather obscure prophesy by Thomas the Rhymer:

When Turing's Tower falls to the land,
Gladsmuir shall be near at hand:
When Turing's Tower falls to the sea,
Gladsmuir the next year shall be.

Gladsmuir was the name the Highlanders gave to their victory at Prestonpans in 1745. Actually it is claimed that the Turing Tower confounded even Thomas the Rhymer and fell both ways simultaneously. Be that as it may, stones from the old tower were used in building the present one, so it still has a right to be known as the Turing Tower.

Sir Samuel Forbes was the second of the new lairds but during his stay the tower was left in ruins. Instead he reconstructed the opulent mansion of Tillery, of which he was also proprietor, in the Udny district.

Foveran eventually passed to John Robertson of Pitmillan, a nearby farm, who was a stocking merchant and sometime Provost of Aberdeen, the second with Foveran connection to hold this office. Mr Robertson first acquired Pitmillan and afterwards Foveran about 1758, on the death of Sir Samuel Forbes. He married a Janet Mitchell, had three sons and a daughter and carried on with his stocking business, which was then very profitable, enabling the family to rebuilt Foveran House and the Turing Tower.

The new mansion was built by the Robertsons in 1771, almost on the site of the old castle. It is a semi-classical structure, with stone steps and balustraded porch entrance to the main hall and staircase of the four-storey building, with rectangular wings of lesser height, forming an open square courtyard and coach entrance at the back. Within the square, tacked on behind the house, and accessible from it by spiral staircase, is an embodiment of the former Turing Tower, a square keep of five flights topped with a flat roof and four baronial round-capped turrets at the corners, surmounted by small spires. But even at this elevation, much higher than the main chimney heads, it is impossible to see over the tree-tops which encircle and isolate Foveran House, and also shelter it from all directions.

The Robertsons occupied Foveran for ninety-nine years, from 1758 to 1857. Andrew, grandson of John Robertson, sold the estate piece-meal: part went to Mr David Gill of Aberdeen, who called his section Blairythan, as it is today, while Kincraig was sold to Mr Alexander Mitchell of Ythan Lodge. Several farms were sold to their occupiers, such as Pitgersie, Pitscaff, Drums, Newtyle, Meikle Haddo, Little Haddo, Kirkhill, Overhill, Frogmore, Dubbystyle, Savoch, Aikenshill etc, and a few of these holdings are still held by family descendants.

The mansion house and 40 acre policies went to Miss Christina Mackenzie, youngest daughter of Roderick Mackenzie of Glack, who bequeathed it to her first cousin, Major-General Roderick Mackenzie of Kintail and Seaforth. In 1878 he married Caroline Sophia, daughter of J A Beaumont of Wimbledon Park, and they had issue, a daughter Florence Mary, born 1879, who lived to be ninety-four, the last resident laird of Foveran, dying there on 26 June 1973.

Attended by an elderly maid, but otherwise severely alone in Foveran House, hemmed in on all sides by the densely wooded grounds, Miss MacKenzie became something of a bird in a gilded cage; a Lady of Shalott in her ivory tower. Very few people intruded upon her serene privacy.

What it was like for a frail old spinster living in that vast mansion is difficult to imagine: what with its damp and ghostly cellars and subterranean stone passages, dark forbidding kitchens with prison-bar murky windows; turretted stairways, labyrinthine corridors; enormous rooms with their cob-webbed paintings and shuttered casements, pillared arcades and piano-key ceilings, marble fireplaces and walls in velvet textured paper—these were for the style and pomp of a former aristocracy—latterly the abode of a lonely old recluse, companion of the cellar rats and the bats of the Turing Tower, the surrounding rookeries of spring her liveliest season, the whiteness of winter the robe of her soul; but perhaps she enjoyed her solitude.

Miss Mackenzie had bathrooms on every landing and electricity was added in 1953, so she was not in darkness and she had every modern convenience, plus a personal courage that was a challenge to anyone in the whole parish to sleep alone for one night in Foveran House when her maid was absent. In her younger days Florence MacKenzie studied music in Germany and on several occasions had tea with Hitler at Berchtesgaden. She was also on good terms with Herr Von Ribbentrop, the pre-war German ambassador to Britain, all of which during the war made her rather unpopular locally, until she realised the error in her sympathies for the Nazi regime.

By the time she died even the walled garden was full of trees, not young saplings that might have seeded themselves in a period of long neglect, but huge gnarled monsters that looked as old as the trees outside the walls, as if the masons had enclosed them from the rest of the wood, which was planted when the house was built.

So it couldn't have been her orchard apples that the local boys were after when they invaded her policies; rather perhaps a curiosity to get a glimpse of Miss MacKenzie herself, but she kept them at gunpoint, the muzzle loaded with barley, and when they came near enough she gave them both barrels from behind a tree, full blast. After her demise the loons roamed freely in the woods, rummaged in her mansion and threw stones at her windows; indeed it seemed that the end was in sight for Foveran House—then oil was discovered in the North Sea and breathed new life into its walls, as has happened with quite a number of our crumbling baronial homes in Aberdeenshire.

I lived for twenty-one years in Foveran parish, and much as I desired to see the 'Big Hoose', I wouldn't have ventured near it while Miss MacKenzie was alive, for such was her reputation in the neighbourhood. The frequent change of tenant at the gate-lodge, where the gardener lived, warned me off for a start, and it stood empty in her last years.

When at last I was privileged to visit the secluded mansion, and while I stood on the lawn where Judge Turin's statue had been, I was attacked savagely by a huge blue dragonfly, perhaps the reincarnation of a former laird—even Miss MacKenzie herself, angered at my trespass on their former grandeur. Even today there are bumps and noises in the night, especially in the Turing Tower, where the maze of little rooms that once housed the servants are now private bedrooms with baths or showers, and there is speculation as to whether the ghost of Miss Florence still haunts her former home. Not that she should be complaining, for although the new proprietors, a Division of Rockall Estates, have stripped and refurbished the house they have left the original design exactly as they found it, inside and out, and much improved on the old mouldering material, even to the magnificent marble fireplaces that have been retained wherever possible. The new wallpaper is pin-prick identical with the old and wood panel replacement cannot be detected. What more could Miss MacKenzie want?

For seven years after her death the mansion was neglected and vandalised. Now there are seventeen bedrooms, all with bath or shower-rooms, radio alarm systems, television and video. What was formerly the ballroom with its coved ceiling is now the tastefully designed Eider Suite for conference and business assemblies. Across the hall is the old library with its Ionic pillars still intact and providing an atmosphere of palatial splendour as the residential dining room. The original dining hall, also on the ground floor, is now the Heron Suite, also used as a conference room, resplendent with its oval end walls and corniced ceiling. On the first floor the former drawing room has been turned into the appropriately named Tern Suite. These conference halls, all with adjoining seminar or syndicate rooms for sub-committee meetings combine classical furnishing with up-to-the-minute facilities, including a comprehensive range of audio visual video equipment capabable of being linked or operated independently.

The work entailed in making this Georgian 'B' listed building solid and weather-proof must have been a sleepless protraction for its designers, and the interiors a severe challenge for the restoration architect; what with its spacious rooms and the honeycomb of old-fashioned closets and recesses which accommodated the servants of a long gone society.

The old trees have been removed from the walled garden, now used as a source for providing vegetables for the hotel kitchens. The expansive front lawn has been reseeded and tea can be had there in parasol shade. Where once there were shoulder-high nettles and docks there are now tennis and croquet courts, a clay-pigeon range, jogging track and golf practice area. While clearing away the weeds and scrub surrounding the house workmen recovered the marble bust of Judge Turing from an old rubbish dump, and this fine figure has also been secured in Foveran Church. In fact the new owners of Foveran House have done everything humanly possible to lay the ghost of the restless Miss MacKenzie. Let us hope they have succeeded.

PETER BUCHAN

Pace-eggs bricht on the yalla san'
In the pale clear sun o' Spring.
Young heids bent in a kysie search
'Mong the rocks far the limpets cling.
Lang fine days wi' their happy ploys,
An' bare feet rinnin' free;
The lilt o' win' throu' wavin' girss,
An' the strong clear call o' the sea.

In visiting Peter Buchan in his home in Peterhead one gets a privileged view of the South Bay and harbour entrance, moreso if he takes you upstairs with the binoculars, where the North Sea is a wide stretch of blue shimmering water, the rock of Skerry in the middle distance, a mile off shore, Buchanness lighthouse to landward, and the gigantic lum of Boddam Power Station adding smoke to the drifting clouds.

'Naething gyangs in or comes oot o' the herber athoot gyan by this windae.' Peter speaks hard core Doric, just as he writes it in his poems, though he can also write good English when he has to. 'I can spick gweed English fin ah hiv till, bit fin it's nae nott ah wid juist be makin' a feel o' masell.'

Directly under us was the harbour control tower, where Peter spent the last six years of his working life, 'as harbour traffic controller', he explained; but now he can watch it at leisure, reflecting on his twenty-eight years at sea.

I sat at the fire on a winter's nicht
When the grun wis fite wi' sna,
An' I watched the lowes wi' their flickerin' licht
Drawin' picters on the wa';
Then deep in the he'rt o' the fire so reid
I saw the face o' a freen—

A barfit loon, wi' a curly heid
An' a pair o' launchin' een;
Then the win' in the lum changed its dreary tune,
An' it hummed a lilt to the launchin' loon:

> Div ye see the P D drifters
> Div ye see them yet ava?
> 'Div ye see the P D drifters,
> Comin' hame fae Stornowa'?'

In his spare time (when he isn't writing) he makes wooden models of the ships he sailed in. He had made four the previous winter, beautifully painted in true marine colours. Behind us on the mantel of the electric fire was a model of the *Twinkling Star*, which he skippered for twelve years, and downstairs the *Lively Hope* was proudly exhibited on a wall cabinet. Upstairs also was an harmonium on which he tinkles at odd moments. 'Oh aye,' he assures me, 'I can tak' a tune oot o' her fin I like!' What he didn't tell me was that he has a fine singing voice for the old Sankey Hymns; throaty and deep chested, considering his slender build, and when accompanied by his wife on the harmonium the lyrics tremble on the slopes of Mount Zion, heart-felt and uplifting, throbbing in the style of the old Negro Spirituals high in the praise of Jehova, more in the spirit of the Mission Hall than that of the Authorised Church of Scotland Hymnary. I learned this from a tape which Peter recorded for the blind, organised by Mr Duncan Simpson, Workshop purveyor of entertainment for the blind, though he has himself been blind since the age of five. I also learned from this tape that Peter Buchan is a marvellous story-teller, rich in the Doric humour, and when reciting his own poems his flow and timing is faultless, his cadences delightful and every word audible. He is a natural for the concert platform, relaxed and unperturbed, casual and at ease in audience response, mostly in explosive laughter, and usually he retires in tumultuous applause. All this is the more astonishing when one realises that only a few years ago Peter Buchan had part of a lung removed, though he has made a rapid and remarkable recovery and has been given the all clear by his doctors. They advised him to stop smoking but he says he can't and he goes in for the mild, low-tar variety.

Back in the house on the stair landing was a polished cabinet library of choice bound books. 'And this is the bedroom', Peter said as I followed him to the far end of the passage. At the lobby window (still upstairs) he pointed to the thickness of the walls, 28 inches, 'and they're clay,' he added, but where it had crumbled he had filled it up with cement. Downstairs there is a framed picture of 'Mount Pleasant' before and after renovation—the old gaunt building with peep-hole windows and brick-topped gable chimneys and tiled roof is contrasted with a slated villa-style modern house with wide sunny windows but still retaining the original structural outline with neat dummy gable chimneys. 'Folk thocht I wis aff ma heid fin I bocht this place,' he mused, 'but since I did it up I hiv hid offers tae buy it—but naething doin'.'

'Did you do it all yourself?' I asked. 'Oh no, but maist o' the navvy wark; shiftin' steens and sic like. Man, there wis some enormous steens in that waa's an' lintels that wid a furnished a Druids' Temple. Och ye've nae idea o' the wark we did.'

'But why "Mount Pleasant"?' I queried, 'when so near the sea,' though I had to admit the view was spectacular with all these oil boats in the bay.

'Weel, it wis like this,' Peter said, 'Fin I wis a bairn we used tae play barfit on the hard rocks doon there on the shore, and there wis naething tae look at but the watter. When we got bigger we managed tae travle oot tae Mount Pleasant at Inverugie yonder whaur athing wis bonnie and saftened wi' colour in the simmer-time. There wis gless windaes in the gairden dykes and when we looked through I niver saw onything sae bonnie; it wis ableeze wi' flooers like the Gairden o' Eden and I said tae masell this maun surely be Heaven. I wis juist a wee loonie mind ye and I have niver forgotten it so I ca'd ma hoose after Mount Pleasant.'

'And your book of poems as well,' I reminded him, for *Mount Pleasant* has been printed six times by different publishers and is again completely sold out. 'I hinna a spare copy left even for masell,' he told me, 'folk comin' tae the door an' siccen et and nae a copy left; we could a selt anither thoosand if we'd printed them.' He has added to the book over the years and it is now quite bulky, 120 pages including photographs and glossary.

'Mount Pleasant' is the one poem Peter Buchan has written purely in English and it is one of my favourites. Four verses will suffice to convey its pastoral fragrance

> And oh! the joy on golden days,
> When summer reigned in robes of green
> To see, a-shimmer in the haze
> The lovely scene.
>
> But Autumn wore the fairest gown
> And bore, thro' fields of tawny sheaves,
> Her vivid shades of red and brown
> To stain the leaves.
>
> Alas her stay was all too brief,
> This maiden with the auburn hair,
> Her passing left the world in grief
> And grey despair.
>
> The child is gone who watched so well
> The fleeting seasons come and go.
> His shadow cannot catch the spell
> Of long ago.

Downstairs in the sunny living room Mrs Buchan prepared afternoon tea and home-baked cakes for us. She is a cheery woman in her sixties with the sun and wind of many summers over the herring barrels in her rosy face. While Peter went to the 'phone I remarked to her that she must have experienced many anxious nights when her man was at sea in a storm. 'Oh aye', she said, 'but he juist has a yawlie noo and he niver gyangs oot over a mile, juist ayont the bey, and I hiv a towie oot at the windae and I can pull 'im in again if he gyangs owre far.'

Peter came back to the window and joined me at tea, his green eyes bright and clear as the sunlight that danced on the water of the bay. Boats were churning out of the harbour at steady intervals. 'Is that the *Courageous*, mither? I can nearly guess by the wurr o' her engine,' his hands full of papers and tea cup. Mither took the spy-glass from the window sill and focused on the heavy motor boat emerging from between the piers. 'Aye, it's the *Courageous*,' she verified, though I could scarcely read the faded print on the bow.

'Aye', Peter agreed, 'she could be deein' wi' a clart o' paint that ane.'

If you can imagine Jimmy Shand a bit younger and with a head of thick grey hair that is my picture of Peter Buchan, the fishermen's Charles Murray. But his smile is more spontaneous and his white leather face lights up with enthusiasm when you speak of poetry or the sea. He was born in Jamaica Street, just up the brae behind the house where he now resides. He went to the Central School in St Peter Street and later attended Peterhead Academy. He left school and went to sea at seventeen when his father died. Some of his experiences at this stage are reflected in the poem 'A Time to Get':

> A growin' loon, a workin' loon
> Ye'll aye cry oot for mait
> An' then ye'll learn the secret knack
> O' keepin't in yer plate.
> The table's showdin' up an' doon
> It's reelin' back an' fore
> An' tattie soup taks queer-like tigs
> It niver took ashore.
> High broadside motion niver moved
> Your mither's kitchen fleer—
> But that was in the steady world
> Ye've left upon the pier.

Once he was thrown overboard and he can't swim. Fortunately the crew managed to rescue him. His biggest fright was in the Pentland Firth in the teeth of a storm when wind and tide were in opposite directions.

> Ye're a' richt if wind and watter are in the same direction, but if wind and tide are fechtin' each ither Gweed help ye. The boatie wis oot o' sicht maist o' the time; ye couldna even see the wheel-hoose, she wis like a submarine awash, and a' because oor skipper wanted tae be hame tae see Peterheid play Deveronvale on the Seterday. A' the ither boats gaed in tae Scrabster herber or the tide changed, but nae oor skipper, an' neen o' the rest o's wis carin' fa Peterheid wis playin'. I fairly thocht I wis done for that time!

I commented that one of his most beautiful poems, a reflection on 'Mount Pleasant', was written in English.

> 'Aye, it's nae bad, but I dinna like writin' verse in English—I prefer the Mither Tongue. I can express masell better in the Doric.' This is obvious of course and he added that although he hadn't made a classical study of the English poets he was familiar with most of them. 'I ken a' aboot Wordsworth and his daffodils and Whittier on nature study but I like tae write aboot folk. My inspiration? No, it's nae fae nater [nature], the sea is a cruel mistress, naething tae extol aboot her grim faced beauties like ye hae on the land; it's folk that I like tae write aboot, character study, a' aboot their faults and foibles, that's what sets me goin'—the human angle. Folk are queer, and the aul'er they get they grou mair queer. Some o' them wid kick ye in the belly fin yer back wis turned. The English poets, weel I niver look at Shakespeare, and for me Charles Murray stauns heid and shooders abeen them a'.

I never mentioned Burns but I know he attends the occasional Burns' Supper locally, though he doesn't address the Haggis. He further admitted that he sometimes read poetry at school when he should have been doing his lessons, and that he also read all the popular boys' fiction of the period: the Ballantyne books, Marryat, Stevenson, Defoe, Charles Kingsley etc.

How and when had he begun writing poetry? 'Aboot 1947 I think, when I had my first poem published in the *Buchannie* (*The Buchan Observer*). We were on the wye hame wi' a catch o' herrin' when the lads aboord began on their pranks and ploys when we were loons and I began tae discover that I had a knack for writin' it doon in verse.'

I asked about his parentage and he said his Deydie (paternal grandfather) was born in Burnhaven of fisher folk. His grannie lived at Buchanhaven as a quine, at the opposite outskirts of Peterhead. When they married the families of each party walked half-way to meet the other. They met at the old ropeworks, now the site of the Bay View Garage overlooking the South Bay, and there they were married, inside the rope factory, where there was plenty of room for a splore and for dancing. 'Their food was tatties and herrin',' Peter explained, 'but of coorse if ye wis a skipper ye wis lookin' for something better, so ye got hard-fish and mustard suace—hairy tatties, ye ken fut I mean, and that wis supposed tae be a luxury.'

His father was also a native of Peterhead but his mother came from Denny. 'She wasna fisher,' he explained, 'her folks were miners and millworkers.'

During the war Peter served in the Barrage Balloon Flotilla, from Sheerness to Scapa Flow: 'Stringin' up balloons tae trap the German airoplanes,' he explained.

The Buchans were married in 1940 and they have two daughters, Anne and Alison. His wife's name before marriage was Agnes Cowe and after a lass in several ports he finishes 'Bird of Passage' with:

> I met a fisher quine at hame,
> A lass I'd kent since she was three;
> But faith, she wasna jist the same,
> For scarcely would she look at me!
>
> Noo that's aa bye—we've spliced richt weel
> An' coorted thirty year an' mair;
> But should she ever say fareweel,
> Wi' clippit wing I'd greet—an' care.

I asked Agnes what she thought of her husband's poetry? 'Oh, it's aa richt by me,' she answered, 'I'm his greatest fan but I'm no critic. It's nae for me tae criticise what he writes. I wid think it above my station in life tae dee that—and efter aa', and here she smiled benignly, 'I'm his inspiration!'

Enquiring on family reaction to his poetry I was informed that they all approved: 'Especially Alison, the youngest quine; she took a degree in English and says I shid write a book aboot my fishin' experiences besides the poetry.'

Since writing the above paragraph this has now been accomplished. For the last year Peter Buchan has been contributing articles and stories on the fishing fraternity to the Aberdeen *Evening Express*, and these are now in book form as *Fit Like, Skipper?* Peter sent his work to the editors in longhand, but such was its quality and expertise in composition that they accepted it, and reader response was generous and applauding. If the editors demurred at all it was because of Peter's nearness to the bone and pruruient humour, sometimes compelling a meeting of staff before printing, though Peter usually won but objected strongly to erasures and shortening of his work. How fortunate he was that the paper accepts his work in longhand, which seldom ever happened with me when I started. Peter now owns and uses an electric typewriter expertly. He insists he is still a poet and never very sure of himself in prose, to which I would reply that he is a natural in either media and vastly entertaining in both, something that was sorely needed from the fishing community, which has never been written up to the extent that farming and countryside have enjoyed. When he left the fishing Peter had fifteen years experience as a travelling agent in fuel oil for the farmers, van provided, motoring all over Buchan and gathering a different type of story, which he can repeat with the same sly humour and casualness he employs with the fisher tales, and he is as much at home on the Buchan roads as a hare in a neep park.

What did he think of the modern generation? 'Weel, they hiv their faults but they made my day juist lately. I canna dee withoot ma boatie ye ken (*Sweet Promise*) an' I wis on ma wye doon tae the shorie fin I met a steer o' school bairns wi' their teachers tae learn aboot the boats and the fishin'. They fair filled the road and I couldna get by so I juist gaed throu the middle o' them. The dominie was there and he cried on me tae stop. He explained tae the bairns that this was somebody they should know: Peter Buchan the poet and they were workin' on some of his poems at the moment. He asked the bairns tae show their appreciation by recitin' one o' my poems. So the whole jing-bang o' them got yokit on 'Kirsty' fae start tae feenish and their Doric was word perfect. It made me rael prood tae hear it and the modern bairns opened ma 'een I can tell ye!'

Twis Kirsty this an' Kirsty that
An' Kirsty needin' sheen!
An' Kirsty's darlin' sheenikies
Maun come fae Aiberdeen.
The verra sark upon her back
Wis sent for, hine awa.
For common dab fae Peterheid
Jist widna dee ava!

But he wasn't so much in favour of the adult generation of modern fishermen. All gone to pride, money, machinery and technology. The human element has gone out of fishing he said and the family ideals had been submerged in 'big business' methods, much like farming where the crofters were concerned. He has written a poem about it in English:

> But the seas still rise to an awesome height
> When the raging gales blow shrill,
> And a faith in things that were made by men
> Is no substitute for skill.
>
> It would seem alas, as the years roll on,
> And the pages of time unfold—
> That the thirst for power is a terrible twin
> To the terrible thirst for gold.

Peter is a member of the Congregational Church and he can stand in for the minister when required. He can quote scripture at length and has strong views on church affairs. He has also been on radio discussions on the fishing industry. His versatility is indeed amazing; he had a spell of teaching at Crimond School just after the war when he was stuck for a job, but with the return of regular teachers from uniform he was obliged to go back to the sea. With Paddy Hat and annorak, beaming eyes and radiant smile Peter Buchan could turn his hand to almost any situation or circumstances confronting him, and he would make a success of it.

I asked him how it was that so much had been written and sung about the farming community and so little about the fisher folk? Folklore and balladry was almost absent from their traditional history. He hadn't thought much about this but agreed with what I said. I suggested that the farming chiels enjoyed a greater social freedom than the fishermen, and a system of six months engagement in work that gave them a license to criticise an employer they had just left. With a skipper it was different and you might still be in his crew when your latest 'cornkister' or 'Wheelhoose Rag' came to light. It is also a fact that while there were several chiels in a chaumer the steersman was mostly alone in the wheelhouse, sternly involved with the mechanics of what he was about, while the others were in their bunks resting between net haulings. Who would want to be domineered by a fiddle or a melodion down below in the throb of the engines and the wash of the sea against the hull?

Peter also agreed that religion might have something to do with
the absence of balladry among fishermen—'Though', he added,
'the fishermen are nae sae religious as they are supposed tae be.'
Crew relationship and mixed marriages were also a factor to be
considered. 'Like kickin' one arse in a village and aa the ithers
dirled!

Apart from Peter Anson and Neil Gunn there was no William
Alexander or Lewis Grassic Gibbon in the fishing world—only
Peter Buchan as the 'Hamewith' of fisher lore.

> Oot-win, caul wi' the threat o' rain,
> Or it might be wi' grey sea fog.
> An' fa's on the bare grey bents the day
> But an' aul' grey man wi' his dog.
> Traivlin' the aul' paths, hearin' soun's
> O' the days that eesed t' be
> In the sough o' win' thru' shiverin' girss
> An' the dreary dirge o' the sea.

ARTHUR GARDINER—
GROCER POET OF DYCE

My mither, doon among the hens
Wis forkin' oot the ketchie grains,
I, in the gairden casual threw
A random tattie tae the blue;
Far and fair it flew indeed
Syne scored a bulls-eye on her heid,
Weel awite I'm tellin' you
I did it aince but widna noo.

The village of Dyce, now a suburb of Aberdeen; airport and largest helicopter station in Europe, is famous for other things besides the Asda Stores and Lawson's sausages. There's Arthur Gardiner's poetry, though sorry to say but few have heard of it. Yet the SPAR grocer of Dyce ranks with the poets of 'Orra-Loon' or 'Hamewith' fame in Doric verse, at least in quality though not in quantity because of his short and harassed existence. In his lifetime his talent rivalled Duffton Scott, but whereas the Inverurie bookseller extolled his art in humorous monologue, Gardiner excelled in song, strumming the Hawaiian guitar in accompaniment; he was also proficient on the flute and organ. A week before his death in 1969 he was entertaining the old-age pensioners in the hall at Dyce, one of the last of our Cornkister-composer minstrels. He died of a heart attack aged fifty-five after suffering fourteen years with thrombosis, rhyming and singing his way through years of illness and anxiety; indomitable and cheerful to the last and busy in many pursuits, refusing to be idle in the most discouraging circumstances. You only have to read his poem to the Bees to appreciate his restless endeavour and his dread of idleness:

> Rakin sair wi' threedy clooks
> In ilka floo'r,
> Tappin' nature's sweetest neuks
> Each fleetin' 'oor.

And here we have the same word thrift in the Doric verse as used by Professor J C Milne in poems of the 'Orra-Loon', almost in abstract, yet clear as a bell to the native ear.

You could say that Arthur Gardiner was another of the Geerie Bards, living but a stone-throw from the river Don, where it flows gently (and as yet unpolluted) round the village and its expanding oil depots and offices, under the golden halo of the Brimmond Hill, crowned in summer with golden whin and broom.

> Sou-westward there, the Brimmond Hill
> Tae soothe a body's e'e,
> The airport on oor windae sill
> Has filled the quarry lee.

And like all Garioch poets Gardiner had his tilt at the Mither Tap, the Don Quixote of Donside:

> A glint o' Scotland braw revealed
> Wad surely moist the e'e
> Gin ye hae drifted far afield
> And hamewith like tae be . . .

For like Charles Murray, Gardiner travelled far from his native heath and knew the heartache of the exile. He served in Egypt and the Middle-East during the Rommel-Montgomery campaign and some of his poems may have been written in homesickness for his native Donside. But even on active service his vision captures the spirit of Lawrence of Arabia on a brow of Egyptian desert, the turban and the flowing robes; the sandstorms the heat

and the relief of the oasis, or the Red Shadow in flight from a hail
of bullets:

> Enchantment dies a speedy death,
> For Desert Songs are but a breath
> Of gay romantic idle claim—
> A figment of the mirage strain.

He served for six years as a driver-mechanic in the rank of private
with RASC.

While I talked to the poet's widow in her home over the shop
at Dyce a jet 'plane from the airport roared over the house and
drowned our conversation. It seemed to capture the spirit of the
man; the dynamic spell of his existence, active to the marrow,
thrustful to the end of his energetic life. But perhaps I was
influenced by a framed photo of the poet in uniform on the sun-
house mantel, and by his lines to the dead airmen, German and
Allied, lying in the old graveyard at Kirkton, in the lee of the
ruined kirk and its Pictish symbol stones on a picturesque knoll
overlooking a wooded crook in the Don valley.

> Alang the Kirkton roadie by
> St Fergus and the Cross,
> Whar frem't and freenly airmen lie
> The conflict's tally loss.

When the jet scream subsided Mrs Gardiner told me her
husband had started serving his time as a grocer at fourteen in
a shop at Dyce, where he worked into manhood and up to the
war years and their marriage. After the war he was offered his
job back but declined it and became a traveller for Brooke Bond
Tea. Some six years later he bought the present site of the Berry-
well Stores and built the shop, then constructed the house on top
of it as his business expanded, with a garage and well tilled garden
at the back, where he busied himself even in his dying hour. He
always had to be doing something, even writing poetry in his few
spare moments, sometimes rhyming his advertisements to sell his
wares, besides amusing his customers, for his publicity
campaigns were a great success in the village.

We've crackers, streamers and balloons,
Forks and knives and mixing spoons,
Baking bowls and roasting tins,
All culinary outs and ins:
Glasses fancy, wine or nip,
Tumblers pleasing to the lip,
Holly wreaths of local make
Circular or crossed in shape;
And further more, we've Christmas trees,
Big or small, just as you please.

Over the 'eident years' of his life Arthur Gardiner scribbled poetry on every subject that gave him thought, and between heart attacks published his best work in book form *The Eident Years*, now a lasting tribute to his memory. To every lover of Doric verse I recommend this slender volume; my only regret being that it is not larger, and that the poet left nothing in manuscript.

Not since Burns' 'Rantin' Rovin' Robin' have I heard a bairn hanselled into the world with such a salutation as Gardiner's Preface to his little book:

A bouncing bairnie spanking new,
Butter widna melt in 's moo,
But what a deevil o' a loon
He cam' tae be in oor hame toon.

And how sad the postscript, and though the poet with a touch of ironic humour is referring to the closure of the old chemical works at Dyce, after ninety-three years of service, little did he know it was also his own epitaph:

The Eident Years begin to fret,
The winds of change are blowing,
E'en while the printer's dye is wet
A grand old oak is going . . .

DEATH OF A FATHER

If the man who turnips cries,
Cry not when his father dies,
'T'is a proof that he had rather
Have a turnip than his father!
Samuel Johnson

It is all such a long time ago, thirty-five years at this time of writing, that had it not been for my diary I should have forgotten most of the details. Looking back over almost half a lifetime it seems a long time to have lived without a father. The house where he lived at the time of his death has been completely erased—not even a foundation stone to mark the site of its existence.

It happened on 9 February 1949, a bad month for our family. When I saw the farmer's wife in the byre I knew instinctively that something was wrong. She asked would I go to the telephone and speak to the village doctor. I went to the office in the farmhouse and picked up the receiver: 'Hello!' I said. The doctor's voice came through in a sympathetic, hesitant manner; yet it was re-assuring just to hear him speak, just to know that he was on the spot (or at least in some farmhouse where there was a telephone) and that something was being done to save my father. Somehow I knew what was wrong. The last time he had been to see us he had said to my wife that he wouldn't come again. That was three weeks earlier and she told me later. Now it had happened.

The doctor was speaking. 'Your father is critically ill. He has had a haemorrhage and a stroke and is almost completely paralysed. Your mother is extremely worried and cannot make up her mind so I want your permission to have your father removed to the infirmary.'

'Where is the haemorrhage?' (stupid question) I asked.

'It's a brain haemorrhage.'

'He'll be unconscious then?'

'Yes, he's unconscious; he doesn't know a thing.'

'Do you think there is a chance doctor?—a chance to save him I mean?'

'Well there is really very little hope, and if he does recover he'll probably be either insane or paralysed for however long he may live; the point is that if I send him to the infirmary there is just the chance that they might save him. But you must give your consent before I can move him, and the sooner he is there the better, while there is still hope.'

'All right doctor, seeing that he's unconscious you can move him right away. Had he been aware of it I couldn't have given my consent because his wish has always been to die at home.'

'I see. Ah well but he's quite unconscious I assure you.'

'O.K. doctor, call the ambulance and I'll be over as soon as I'm dressed.'

'Hurry then, don't bother to dress!'

I told my boss what the trouble was and hurried home on my bicycle as fast as I could. I washed and dressed as fast as ever I did in my life, all the time relating to Jane about my father's condition, and when I had swallowed a cup of tea I barged off again. I cycled the three miles in the rain and arrived at the cottage at the same time as the ambulance. The doctor was waiting and my father lay on the kitchen bed in a stricken state. He was twisting his head from side to side on the pillow, and every now and then passing his right hand across his brow. I spoke to him but he made no answer. Assured that he was quite unconscious I assisted the doctor and the ambulance driver in rolling him into a blanket and on to the stretcher by the bedside. I helped my mother into the ambulance beside my father and climbed in myself, the driver slamming the door behind us, and the doctor waving goodbye in the same instant. The ambulance windows were of frosted glass so that I had no idea how fast we

were going or where we were on the road. All the time we seemed
to be tearing on at tremendous speed. I could hear the water
swishing the mudguards and underneath the chassis. Always my
father crossed his brow with his hand and opened and compressed
his lips as if he were thirsty or wanted to speak. Continually he
threw off the blankets and it was all that both of us could do to
keep him covered. Once he groped for my mother's hand and
caught it, held it tight; then he caught mine and I felt a slight
squeeze, but only for a moment for his hand went back to his head
again. Perhaps it was a physical reaction to the subconscious, an
involuntary action which seemed to indicate that the mind was
still trying to do its job despite the flow of blood released on it.
It was a touching moment which almost brought tears to my eyes.
My mother kept repeating to me that she hoped he would get
better. After what the doctor had told me I had no real wish for
it. I had no desire to see my father awaken to such misery as he
had foretold. One death of this sort was quite sufficient for one
man to bear. Thankfully he was spared the knowledge of it. My
mother's tears fell on his face when she bent over him from the
seat at his head. As often as she covered him up he persistently
threw the blankets aside when he raised his arm to his head. He
was beyond her comfort now and it filled me with sadness when
I realised it. Over and over again she told me of his last moments
of consciousness: How he had got up first as usual and sat in his
armchair, smoked his pipe and started to put his clothes on; how
his mouth had twisted when he uttered speech, and all he had
managed to say was 'There's something wrang wi' me the day
'uman; something wrang wi' me the day!' She had risen and
dragged him to the bedside but was unable to lift him on to it.
She left him sitting on the rug with his head against the dresser
while she ran for her neighbour across the road. Between them
they managed to lift him on to the bed. They gave him cream
chocolate and though he couldn't chew it melted and ran down
his throat. It seemed to revive him for he found his voice again
and opened his eyes. They asked if he knew them. First the
neighbour woman asked and then my mother. When our
neighbour asked he said: 'Aye, I ken ye fine, ye're Mrs Robbie!'
and when my mother asked he said: 'Aye, my wee wifie!' It was
the last time he ever spoke to her, the last words she was ever to
hear from his lips 'My wee wifie!'—what he had called her

from my childhood. They had sent for the doctor and he had 'phoned me immediately. My mother was sad now and I could do nothing to comfort her.

After an hour, but what seemed a prison sentence, I knew by the noise that we were in the bustle of city traffic. The ambulance seemed to swerve and jolt and there was the grind and screech of brakes and the shrill tone of the clarion horn. Finally we stopped and the driver got out and opened the back door. We were at the main entrance of the hospital and almost immediately an orderly appeared with a trolley on rubber tyres. The driver took the trolley and pulled my father's stretcher on to it from the van. He pushed the trolley through the entrance and waved us on to follow him. He walked extremely fast, so that we had to run almost to keep up with him, my mother catching my sleeve lest she should fall behind.

We swept along the seemingly endless corridor in muffled silence, nurses and students in white coats meeting us on either side, and innumerable patients and orderlies coming and going in both directions, all gliding along as if it were a dream, and the trolley sweeping ahead of us in urgent majesty. The smell of ether and disinfectant put all sorts of disconcerting thoughts into my mind, one chasing the other as it were for supremacy, until I was forced to banish them wilfully, and to keep my attention on the trolley. There were openings to left and right and flights of steps that disappeared in a curve towards the roof, an arrow painted on the wall at the foot of each staircase and the numbers of the wards they led to. There were windows on both sides of the corridor, each one framing a different view of the hospital buildings as we flashed along. The floor was paved in black and white diamond squares and the walls and ceilings were painted a dull yellow. The stairs looked like polished stone and everything conveyed the impression of cold but efficient austerity.

At last the trolley stopped and the driver pressed a lift button. The doors slid apart and we crowded inside around the trolley. The doors closed automatically and we had the buoyant impression of being borne upwards. The lift stopped with the faintest jolt and the doors opened and we emerged on another landing. We were met by a doctor and nurse and they took the trolley from our driver and disappeared into a ward. The driver gave us a word of parting and went back the way he had come, while we stood nonplussed at the entrance to the ward. The rain had stopped and the sun began to shine through the tall windows, indeed it seemed as if he was smiling on us through the tears of the angels.

For half-an-hour we stood there, too anxious to sit down or to talk much. Now and then we peeped into the ward. There was a row of beds along each side and a wide passage up the centre. Every bed had a patient, some were sitting up reading, others lying flat, and a ward sister was writing at a table at the far end. My father's bed was on the right nearest the door and there were white screens all around it. Some of the patients were looking towards it and whispering to each other across their beds. There was a noise of talking along the corridors and the distant clatter of dinner plates. All else was silent.

At last a doctor appeared from the ward and beckoned us into an office across the corridor. 'Sorry to keep you waiting', he said. He was a man about thirty-five, lean and heavily tanned, and he wore a white coat like all the others we had seen. He motioned us to be seated and drew a chair for himself towards a desk against the wall. A ledger lay open in front of him, and having lit a long slender pipe he took a pen and began to write in it. Now and then he turned to us for information. 'How old was the patient? Was he a nervous man? What was his employment?' He furnished us with a visiting card and directed us to a conservatory where he said we could wait for a while—and later perhaps we could go into the ward. Before the doctor left us I asked him if there was any hope. 'Well', he said, 'his chances are very slender. Had your father been a younger man we might have managed to stop the bleeding, but at his age the arteries are hard and less easy to heal. I have extracted a pint of fluid from the base of the spine to ease the pressure on the brain. Meantime it is all we can do and you must await further developments. I'm sorry', he added with a note of sympathy. He accompanied us along the corridor to a seat with other visitors.

A girl from the dining room appeared with a tea trolley, a cuppa that was most welcome in the circumstances, and we sat and talked and waited for two whole hours before the doctor returned for us.

I was almost afraid to enter the ward because I heard my

father's breathing from the door. We went behind the screens and looked at him. The doctor closed the screens and left us. We were alone with a dying man on his gurgling trip to the grave.

My father's breathing frightened me, a hollow sepulchral rasping as if a rusty chain was being pulled up and down his throat. My mother spoke words of endearment and comfort but she might as well have spoken to a stranger. She wept over him and begged him not to leave her. What with my father in the throes of death and the plight of my mother I was brought to tears myself. The inevitability and the finality of death suddenly dawned on me. But I pulled myself together and tried to face it bravely. After all I had always treated my father kindly and I had nothing to repent beyond parting with him. Of what my mother's feelings were, or of what she was thinking I could only guess. I opened my father's eyes with my thumb and they were fixed with a terrified stare at the ceiling. There was no prospect of heaven in his looks, only the blind terror of death. His heart thumped against his rib cage and jerked his head slightly with every quickening beat. He had ceased to move his hands and they lay by his sides under the blankets. He seemed far too hot and blobs of perspiration gathered on his brow. I slackened his shirt at the neck and pulled down the bed-clothes. It was then I noticed how thin he was, like some of the press photos from the German concentration camps, yet I knew he had always eaten well—it was no reflection on my mother's cooking. He was emaciated to the bone, a quivering skeleton almost, and the sight of him filled my heart with pity.

The hours slipped away and the chain corroded in my father's breast. His breathing became a steeplechase, halting and pitiful to watch. Puss reached his mouth and almost choked him, then ran from the corners of his mouth to the pillow. Respiration was suspended for a moment, so that we bent closer, thinking it was the end, but an involuntary cough set him breathing again. Doctors swabbed his throat and pulled up elastic phlegm with a tongs. I turned my head away. My poor father! Yet I had some consolation in the knowledge that he felt nothing and that everything was being done for him that could be done. His wiry body and magnificent heart put up a stubborn fight, prolonging the struggle and wringing our hearts; yet we stood by, soon the blood would be exhausted through the punctured artery and the heart would stop.

Meanwhile I telephoned relatives, my aunt Josephine and uncle Joss in particular, whom my mother wanted near her at the end. My sister was too far away to be summoned so I wrote to her from Archibald's house in the city. There I shaved and had supper with Archibald and Vera (my wife's sister) and returned to Forresterhill infirmary. About nine o'clock my aunt and uncle came in and I telephoned my boss to let Jane know how my father was. There were some further slight convulsions caused by difficult breathing, when at times he seemed to choke, but apart from that my father lay quite still towards the end. He passed away peacefully at 1 a.m. on 10 February, seventeen hours after he had taken ill. Someone passed the coverlet over his face and I led my mother away weeping and shaken. Life for us would go on but for my father the world had ended.

That night we slept with my uncle and aunt in their home at Laurencekirk, where they drove us with their car after midnight. The hills were white with snow, beautiful and serene in the silver moonlight. White frost glistened everywhere and a cold wind rushed against the windscreen. My mother and her sister talked in the back seat and I sat in front beside my uncle Joss. Trains rumbled all through the night and I heard the Mearns clocks strike every quarter. Across the passage I could hear my mother sobbing in my aunt's bedroom. I slept little until morning. After breakfast with the family I wrote out a press notice of my late father's death and quite unwittingly I forgot to give my mother's maiden name, an omission which offended her family when I met them at the funeral. Uncle Joss read it over but he made no comment at the time, perhaps because it didn't directly concern him.

Later in the day he drove us back to Aberdeen to the infirmary, to collect my father's clothes and our blankets. We were conducted to the office in the centre of the building, where a host of typists were tapping at their machines, and which was most exquisitely furnished, and the vestibules and arcades adjoining it magnificently designed and carpeted. Here we had to sign some papers but refused to have a post-mortem examination. My father suffered from no life-long malady which a post-mortem could reveal as a benefit for other sufferers. Besides it would have been very much against his wishes. All night he had lain on a cold slab in the mortuary under the building, the very thought of which would have terrified him out of his reason while he lived.

I registered the death in the city and later returned home with my mother. My father's corpse arrived at the cottage at Cutty-hill, Rora, in the undertaker's van about five o'clock in the after-noon. We set two tables together in the benroom and arranged the coffin on top. The coffin was polished avon, with brass name-plate and handles and purple tassels along the sides. The under-takers unscrewed the lid and propped it against the fireplace. My father made a pleasant corpse. All the lines and wrinkles were gone from his face, and his countenance was more peaceful and youthful than it had been since ever I could remember him. Death had erased all his worries and morbidities and at last he was at peace with the world. The physiognomal transformation was comparable with a framed picture over the mantelpiece which was taken when he was twenty-one, a smart slim youth with close cropped head and small eyes, a trim moustache over a mouth of great composure and the whole face voluminous of perfect serenity of mind and temperament. Such a contrast to the man we knew in later years; a man whose face became the shop-front of misery; whose eyes became pinholes that wouldn't admit the light to his brooding soul; a man ground down with work and years of misfortune before his time, and who seemed to be looking into his own grave for whole days at a stretch. But he was never the one to complain: mother had always been the hypochondriac and did all the girning, yet she survived him by twenty years.

I went to see the sexton in the evening. We lit a lamp beside the bier all night and I sprawled most of the time in an armchair beside the kitchen fire. Mother occupied the kitchen bed but neither of us slept very much. The wind moaned under the doors of the old cottage and it was eerie with the thought of my father lying dead in the bedroom.

Next morning I cycled home to see how Jane was making out and to consult my boss about getting time off to arrange the funeral. He gave me the rest of the week and I said I would compensate with the same number of days deducted from my summer holidays. Back at the cottage there were several con-dolences and one in particular from my bookish friend—John James Sangster, who always signs himself 'Jay-Jay'.

My Dear Davie,
    You have had a severe jolt and a very great loss. To lose one's

father is to lose part of one's self, but such is the condition of nature.

Although I do not know your mother, I feel deeply for her at this sombre hour, and I trust she has the strength to bear the shock and separation with the fortitude she has hitherto possessed.

It is lamentable that your father had not longer of his days of well-earned retirement from labour. Often and much I have written you, but, for once I cannot find words to adequately express my sympathy for you and yours in grief.

'God grant all of you the serenity to accept the things you cannot change.'

Yours Most Sincerely, Jay-Jay.

We bought wreaths and made general preparations for the funeral, like hiring a bus for the mourners. I was glad to see my sister. There were a great many visitors and sympathisers. Some of the women broke down when they talked to my mother. It was one of the longest week-ends of my life and we had the funeral on Monday, 14 February 1949.

On that occasion I was rebuked by two of my mother's brothers for omitting her maiden name from the death notices in the press. They cut the tassels they were holding when they lowered the coffin into the grave and kept them as souvenirs. They did a pub crawl on the way back from the cemetery and said they had poured whisky on my father's flowers, their way of giving him a good send-up. Back at the cottage Selby actually held my nose while Simon poured some whisky into my mouth. This was their reaction to my teetotalism for at that time in my life I never touched drink. Bernard Shaw and J Arthur Rank were my heroes and I stuck to their principles of total abstinence. Of course my uncles didn't know about this and they wouldn't have understood it if they had. They made a real soak of it far into the night and turned solemnity into an excuse for jubilation. I said nothing but I thought it was disgraceful on my father's burial day. One would have thought it was a wedding they were attending and it showed little respect for mother's feelings. Simon kept repeating that my father had been 'one of God's bairns'. They went roaring away in their car in the small hours, singing at the top of their voices.

The following Saturday we hired a taxi and motored to my father's grave at Old Deer. He had nine wreaths, three of them real flowers, and the doucing of whisky seemed to have preserved them for they were beautiful. Mother knelt over the flowers and murmured these lines:

> Thy purpose Lord we cannot see
> But all is well that's done by thee.

She wept bitterly and Jane and I turned our heads away. It is all very sad and touches one deeply.

I settled with Burnetts of Mintlaw about the hire of the bus and the hearse on the way home. We played cards in the evening. We had aunt Mabel (Jane's sister) with her two boys and also my cousin Mary. Time has feet of lead on these occasions. My mind was like a ship before a gale and my thoughts would anchor nowhere.

On the first day of my return to work I came home exhausted from the turnip field, Dr Johnson's words ringing in my ears:

> If the man who turnips cries,
> Cry not when his father dies . . .

I was glad to sit still in the evening. When death comes to one's hearthstone we lay aside our trophies. I had to force myself even to read the newspapers and all my hobbies were laid aside. Death is indiscrimating and life is cruel. But such a day it had been, and the strongest gale of my experience ended when the stars came out. Haystacks were crumbled down to the ground in the high wind and fodder was blown across the fields like sea spray. Corn stacks were dishevelled and corn sheaves were leaping about in the stackyards like salmon over the waterfalls. Bales of straw were toppled about as if by unseen hands. The trees moaned under the strain and some were broken down or uprooted. Telegraph wires quivered like hairs and hen-arks were scattered about the fields like children's play blocks in a nursery.

> But if the man who turnips cries . . .

And then the farmer who owned my mother's cottage threatened her with eviction unless she returned to milk his cows. This is the sort of thing that happens when the breadwinner is taken away, even though he is a pensioner.

> Cry not when his father dies,
> 'T'is a proof that he had rather
> Have a turnip than this father!'

THE RELUCTANT RAT RACE

Lo, this only have I found, that God hath made man upright; but
they have sought out many inventions. Ecclesiastes 7-29.

Some people have the idea that mechanisation on the land was
accomplished within a decade, or even less, say within a few
years, when in fact it was a very slow process and covered nearly
half-a-century, from around 1920 to 1970, and is still with us in
1984, though the momentum has gone out of it. No exact dates
can be given, because there is no precise beginning or end to
invention and the period of experimentation is difficult to deter-
mine. Throughout the period of my own experience on the land
I have noted down when new machines made their first appear-
ance in my own area, and in this manner we trace the changes
that eventually revolutionised farming patterns.

During the First World War we had experimental ploughing
by steam-traction with the winch system but it never became
popular and should not be judged as a progressive step in
mechanised farming. There was also experimental ploughing
with an early type of paraffin traction in the 1920s but again it
never became common practice. Drag ploughs on wheels was a
legacy from horse ploughing and was adapted for tractor work
in the late 1930s but with little enthusiasm. It was not until
the Ferguson outfit developed the hydraulic lift system in the
late 1940s that tractor ploughing really got under way, almost

contemporary with the mechanical muck loader. The new power-lift made better use of the existing propulsion shaft and with the universal pinion-joint adapted the tractor for most of the new implements that were coming on the market. The universal joint, or 'Hardy-Spicer' as the tractormen called it, gave them complete manoeuvreability in the field, and when lift and power-shaft were synchronised from ground level they could tackle anything.

But let us begin in 1928 when I saw the first tractor employed in farm work. It was a four-cylinder Fordson but all it did was drive the threshing mill in the barn and the farmer would never have thought of hitching it to a cart or plough. My next five farms were still worked by horses but in 1934 I moved to Newseat of Peterhead where I saw my second tractor, a Rushton, but still only used for roadwork, pulling four-wheeled waggons that had formerly been hauled by traction-engines, loaded with coal or manure and was never seen in the fields. The horse was still the predominant beast of burden, but in 1938 when I flitted to my eighth farm, Ednie of St Fergus, I saw a tractor make its first encroachment on the equestrian domain. This was hay-sweeping, when a broad wooden-slatted sledge was fitted to the front axle of the Fordson and used for sweeping hay coles across the fields to the stack-yard, an occupation which had always been done by the horses with a tow-rope or hand-held hay gatherer, not unlike the 'Tumbling-Tom' which was for swath gathering. But after the hay-making the tractor was put in the garage again and the horses resumed their accustomed routine, even pulling the binders in harvest.

Next year the war started and with the clamour for more culti-vation a new plough was bought and the Fordson was taken out of the garage and yoked to it. Over the next four years two new Oliver tractors were purchased and sheep pasture that had been in grass for a hundred years was brought under the plough. Rubber was scarce in the war years and one of these Olivers (supplied under the Lease Lend agreement with America) had iron wheels, so that it couldn't go on the roads, and with increased acreage in cultivation there was no reduction in staff or in equestrian horse-power. But 1940 was the last harvest in my experience tackled by the horses; henceforth the existing trailer binders (driven by ground wheel motivation) were fitted with shorter drag-poles for tractor use. The next step was the power-drive binder, propelled by the power-shaft on the tractor, and the cutting-bar width was extended from 4 and 4½ feet to 6 feet, in some cases 7 feet. But the 7 foot machines 'bit off more than they could chew' and overloaded the sheafing board and the binding and knotter mechanism and were never popular.

There was more to driving a binder than just sitting on the driver's seat. It was an exacting, complicated and excessively concentrated operation, for besides guiding the horses the driver had to adjust the various levers for the changing condition of the crop and for the elevation of the ground. In fact I believe it gave the latter day horsemen their first experience of the mechanisation which was to follow. It was 'forrit for short and back for lang stuff' in manipulating the lever to adjust the string in the middle of the sheaf when it entered the binding mechanism, otherwise you would have a row of 'umbrella' sheaves tied too close to the ears or shear, which were a sore trauchle for the stookers and untidy for stacking, loosing corn stalks all over the place. The driver also had to adjust the platform elevation by a lever at his side, a shorter stubble in lea crop to increase straw yield and a slightly ranker stubble on 'clean lan'' (after turnips) so as not to damage the young grass and clover that had been sown in with the oats or barley in the spring. The raising and lowering of the reels for swathing the standing corn on to the travelling canvas on the platform was another exercise, and the reels could also be moved backwards and forwards to suit the height of the crop, very low and backwards over the cutting blade for short crop and higher and foward for ranker stuff, otherwise you threw it too far back on the platform for proper binding. The butting board for tidying the shear of the sheaf at the front of the binder also required attention, and of course if the twine broke you had to know how to thread your machine.

As with motor cars there were different makes of binders with different controls and this was another complication. With some machines the sheafing-board slide might be 'back for short and forrit for lang stuff', and with all the levers in different positions it took a bit of practise to master them. There were binders with the twine cannister at the front while others had it under the driver's seat at the back; some had the cranking handle at the side but most had it at the rear, and the Albion was distinguishable

distinguishable from most other makes in that it had single reel or flail struts while most others had twin struts. The Albion was a heavier machine and always required three horses to pull it, while the lighter machines, like the Deering or McCormick with a four-foot cutting-bar could be hauled by two horses. Another difference was that though most binders were left-hand cut there were others with the cutting gear on the right-hand side, which was very useful when two binders were employed in the same field with a lodged crop lying one way; the two machines could tackle it from opposite sides cutting one way, free-wheeling back along the stook lanes to take off another bite. The horse binders were all ground motivated from the heavy driving wheel under the chassis, all chain and shaft propulsion, even to the rollers inside the canvasses and the rod to the cutting blade, so that when the horses stopped everything stopped and you had to use the cranking handle to empty the binder for a fresh start. The introduction of the power-drive binders saved you the trouble of using the cranking handle. Even though you had stuck in a lying hole and the binder choked full of straw you could set the machinery in motion from the tractor to clear the canvasses. From the farmer's point of view the tractor binders were a disadvantage in that two men were required on the job in place of one, a man on the tractor and another on the binder, about the only instance of machinery increasing labour costs, and as the horse pace was just about right for binder work there was little increase in speed. But because he didn't have to steer, the man on the binder had a much easier job than he had on the old horse-drawn machines, and with a wider cutting bar he was biting off a bigger mouthful.

It was at Ednie also that I had my first experience with silage; not grass ensilage but consisting of green corn, beans and peas, stored in concrete towers to a height of seventy feet, and not to be confused with the modern corn silos; some of these defunct monuments may still be observed in the farming countryside. But their use required as much man-power as a portable threshing operation and very few persisted with them beyond the war years. The only mechanical equipment employed with tower ensilage was the chopper and blast and the traction-engine driving it to convey the green crop to the turrets of the tower, wherein it fell from a chute in a heavy shower and was trampled underfoot by a couple of inmates. But all the field work was manual, gathering and loading the tares from the swaths laid down by the horse reapers. It had not been devised as a labour-saving expedient but as an alternative to turnip feeding of cattle in a snow storm, or when the turnip crop failed, besides being a nutritious diet which could be fed with turnips alternately, sliced turnips for breakfast and silage for supper, or the other way round, which ever menu suited the routine, for the mid-day meal had lately been discontinued in the bovine cuisine. The chief snag was the lack of water in the steadings to balance the fibrous diet, while cattle were still chained and individual drinking bowls had not been fitted in the byre stalls, something which had not been required with the all too succulent turnip, the juicy apple of the bovine world. Grass ensilage is beset with the same problem but with cattle loose in courts water is easily laid on.

Tower ensilage belonged to the horse era and lost favour to pit ensilage with the coming of the tractors. It was a marriage of convenience that revolutionised animal husbandry, especially with the self-feed expedient, which enabled farmers to house more cattle with a minimum of human involvement. The old hand-feeding, barrow-wheeling cattlemen of my own day are all dead and buried, and except for showyard purposes the beef-producing stockmen as such are now non-existent. Anyone who can get on a tractor nowadays can feed the livestock and there is no longer any pride or reputation in the job—other than seeing how quick and easy it can be done. Where beef-producing stock-men do still exist they are catering for something like 200 head of cattle compared with the forty odd in the old days of byre husbandry, and in the process have enlisted tractor facilities in feeding and removal of sludge, relevant to the drudgery of the past when it was accomplished with barrows and the carrying of 'neep skulls'.

Compared with the factory bred pig, the mass incubated chicken and the battery hen in cages, the ox has fared better in the machine age. He is still condemned to die by execution but he is no longer a byre prisoner with a chain about his neck throughout the winter months. For six months at a stretch these animals couldn't lick themselves or lie down properly on their cobbled or concrete beds, thinly coated with straw, mostly with-out water or fresh air, so that they sweated in their own metabol-ism and suffered the itch of skin irritation or vermin, inhumane discomforts that grew worse as they got fatter, in neglected cases the chains embedded in their necks, dependant as always on the conscientiousness of the cattleman looking after them or the vigilance of the farmer. Now that the chains have been loosed from their necks the animals enjoy a new freedom in natural exercise and fresh air which was denied them in the old claustrophobic existence, and they can grow a winter coat on their hides as protection against the elements indoors or out, and they can chew the cud contentedly or go to sleep comfortably on their own warm dunghill, what in winter you might call the open-prison system for the poor dumb brutes who have harmed no one.

But even in animal husbandry the changes were halting and indecisive. For years the farmers had threatened to turn our cattle loose and send us to work in the fields. But for the persistent belief that byre-fed cattle killed out heavier for the butcher than those nurtured in courts the disbanding of cattle may have come sooner. Indecision sometimes reached crisis point on a mart day when the byres were emptied for the fat ring. Before leaving for the sales the farmer left instructions with the grieve to break up the concrete stalls in the byre for a refill of loose store cattle. But at the mart he was so impressed with the weight of his byre-reared stock over that of cattle from existing courts that he telephoned his wife to cancel the order he had given his grieve. Fortunately the grieve had been hindered with something that morning and hadn't yet got started with the heavy hammer in the byres. This went on for years and was by no means an individual case. But with continued wage increases the change came eventually and very few experienced beef-producing cattlemen now exist as such but cater also for breeding stock, a sideline which has been accentuated by the import of continental breeds, like the big-boned French Charolais, Limousin and the German Simmental. And the cattlemen nowadays are just as mechanically minded as the rest of them and can take their turn with the others in the fields.

Having brought the meat and livestock situation up to refrigeration date, and having got rid of all excess cattlemen, let us go back to the end of the war years to see what was happening in the mechanical world. At that time I was working at Cairngall farm, near Longside in Aberdeenshire, and here they had got the length of a D2 diesel caterpillar tractor but still retained a pair of horses, as most other farmers did, and the reason for it was drill-splitting, or more appropriately drill-closing, mostly in potato planting, as the practice in turnip growing had been overcome years before with surface dunging in late autumn. It was an exercise that the tractors never really mastered; even with narrow tread adjustable-gauge rear wheels they could not be adapted for drill closing where potatoes had been bucket planted. No machine could match a horse walking on the crown of an earth drill, so as not to bruise or dislodge the potatoes in the bottom between the drills, and a pair of horses pulling a drill-plough was the correct method for this purpose.

By 1949 however, because of the now advanced precision robot potato planting machines, drill closing was no longer necessary and the horses were finally disposed of. By the early nineteen-fifties very few horses remained on the larger farms and by the end of the decade even the crofters had got rid of them. A point worth noting here is that because of the increased death rate of horses from grass-sickness the advent of the tractor was a salvation in motive power for agriculture. Even in 1984 this terminal equestrian illness has not been eradicated and is still in evidence at riding schools or where a number of horses are congregated. It is not infectious but usually the prime of the animals fall victim to the disease.

When the horses went I remember recording it in my diary, adding 'presumably we are now fully mechanised.' But of course we were not. It was only a foot (or rather a tyre) in the door, eventually round our necks to throttle our existence as a man force on the land. But so far there had been no reduction in staff and we thought that the machines were a great boon because they were making life easier for us on the land. We were still required all the year round to handle the harvest and threshing operations, for potato gathering, turnip pulling and general duties, all of which would be mastered by the machines eventually. But we could not forsee this and to borrow Harold MacMillan's later pun 'we never had it so good' physically and even our pay was rising to an industrial level in society. Cottar houses were being fitted with bathrooms for key men in the machine age; for grieves and dairy cattlement and our turn would come. A great many of these grant-aid houses are now standing empty or leased to outsiders but even the farmers could not have guessed this outcome of affairs in the Fools' Paradise we momentarily enjoyed.

As general workers we now had the half-day off on Saturdays like the tradesmen and no one was required at week-ends to look after the horses. Tractormen were required to put in a fixed number of hours on garage or maintenance work but so long as they looked after their machines there were no strict rules. Our yearly holiday was increased from three working days to a week on full pay, though of course we had lost our Term and feeing-market days but we still got a day off at the New Year. From the ten and later 9½ hour day worked by our fathers our working hours were reduced to 8¾ hours daily, later to 8½ hours and 8 hours per day for three months in winter. Stockmen were slightly better paid and were obliged to work longer hours in winter, including week-ends, with one week-end clear a month. I worked every week-end in winter because the farmer didn't like strangers in the byre. He said it upset the cattle and I was paid the modern equivalent of £1.25 for one week-end out of four, involving nearly nine hours of work, and the other three week-ends I worked for nothing. Twenty years were to elapse before we got the five-day week and I enjoyed only a month of it before I left the farms in 1971. For many years however we were required to work a ten-hour day for six weeks in harvest with no increase in wages. Farmers on the Agricultural Wages Board stipulated these conditions and enlisted a lot of sympathy from independent members in the matter of bad harvesting conditions. The combine-harvester was to end all that however and overtime payment became compulsory. By the late nineteen-fifties and early nineteen-sixties there was an abundance of overtime and those who indulged in it could afford to run a motor car. The grieves and dairy cattlemen were the first to acquire a car but most of us caught up with them eventually; moreso when staff was reduced in the late nineteen sixties and overtime became a free for all and farmers couldn't get enough of it.

It was at Cairngall farm in the mid nineteen-forties that I had my first experience of pit ensilage, the catepillar tractor clambering over the rising mound of grass with a weight and pressure that made my tiny footprints seem ineffective when I had trampled the tower silo. It was explained to me however that with the broad cleats of the catterpillar track the pressure per square inch was the same, though I could hardly believe it, for the tractor was nearly two tons and I was only eleven stone. It was the only time

I ever saw a caterpillar tractor used for pit-rolling. Most farmers preferred wheel pressure on the pit silos and rubber-tyred tractors are used nowadays. Silage making has always been a bit of a mystery to me, but it appears that constant pressure is required on the grass during the operation to extract oxygen and raise a temperature that would boil an egg to ensure fermentation and better results. Pit rolling always seemed such a waste of time— running back and forth with a tractor on the same pit for days on end (even when no fresh grass was being added to it) until you nearly fell asleep on the job and could have killed yourself on the drop over the sides. But as overtime it was a lazy way of making a fast buck.

Silage effluent (bree from the pits) choked our drains in winter with a growing fungus that filled the pipes, sometimes the whole length of a field until the drain reached an open ditch, and I can sympathise with the environmentalists when they objected to the effluent getting into fresh water streams, for I do believe it could poison fish and prove a health hazard for the community. Rods could scarcely pierce the fungi and we had to dig out the pipes at given distances to get rid of it. The answer I believe is stone soakaways or sludge pits to accommodate seepage from the silage ramps, and these cess-pools have to be emptied periodically by tanker suction.

Grass ensilage began with the green-crop loader, a giraffe like machine which was pulled along the swaths of cut grass which it licked up with revolving prongs and carried it on an elevator well above the cart and dropped it for a man building the load, the whole contraption hauled by a tractor way out in front. This machine persisted for over a decade until it was replaced by the modern forage harvester, a travelling chopper-blast machine which makes a whirlwind of man's laborious efforts to load a huge caged-in cart in about fifteen minutes, another reason for depopulation of the land force.

But in 1950 on one of the more progressive Buchan farms we were still cutting corn with power-driven binders and stooking and stacking corn sheaves—very little barley at that time. Stack-building was still a skilled job and much of the harvest still depended on the skill and reputation of the builders. The occasional combine-harvester appeared in the district, hired from a contractor by some individual farmer who had a field of oats severely lodged by adverse weather conditions. The combine licked up every straw and left a tidy stubble. It would have taken a squad of men a whole week struggling with scythes to compete with what that machine accomplished one sunny Sunday after-noon—moreso, for it was all threshed forbye, and a lot of sight-seers witnessed the operation. This machine was of the sack-filling type, before the tanker with auger for cart loading, and the oats had all to be carted away to a kiln for drying. So far we never imagined it as a coming threat to our jobs and livelihood—in fact it seemed a Godsend.

In the North-East of Scotland the combine-harvester was re-garded as a novel experiment which would never succeed in our notorious climate. And but for the resort to barley growing and the innovation of a short stalk early ripening variety of this cereal I am doubtful if the combine would have had the same success. It was marvellous what could be done with a binder on a matur-ing crop of oats while you waited for the dead ripe conditions essential for combine harvesting.

In farming statistics the combine-harvester must surely be the most expensive and least used piece of equipment in the book, and in operation the most vulnerable to inclement weather in recovering investment charges, even when hired out to neigh-bours. Imagine a factory manager installing machinery he could use only one month in the year (and that sporadically) and for the other eleven months it rusted in idleness. He would go frantic. He might have to contend with one labour strike in five or ten years but this one happens every year, so all things are not equal, least of all at the bank where overdrafts accumulate. Set against this is the phenomenal reduction in all labour costs, a gamble which, through necessity rather than choice can only become viable in long term investment.

There was a time when the initial cost of a combine would have covered the contemporary wage bill for the greater part of a year, perhaps more, so for the less enterprising, or for those with a worrying overdraft, the only way to use them was by hiring from a contractor, a system which entailed considerable periods of waiting until the contractor could handle your crop, since every-body was harvesting at the same time, and you had to wait your turn on the list, even though you had booked a year in advance, and in this prolonged interval you either lost the best of your grain yield or missed the best weather or fell victim to both misfortunes. One windy night can mean disaster to a dead ripe crop of corn or barley, especially barley where the whole head drops off, whereas with oats only single ears are lost. The old binders could be used on a crop just prior to ripening, when the danger of stripping is minimal, and the crop matured in stook and cornstack. But not so with the combine which is an all purpose machine.

The hiring system from contractors was a factor which split the community farming practice in Britain right down the centre. Perhaps it is one of the reasons for harvest failures in Communist Russia, and it drove British farms to private enterprise and individual ownership, perhaps with some encouragement from the banks. Contracting is still practised but on a scale much reduced from the initial onslaught of combine harvesting when it was 'deil tak' the hindmost'—and sometimes he did!

The installation of drying plant and grain storage facilities was another extravagant outlay before combine harvesting could be adopted wholeheartedly. The alternative was the transport of grain from the farm to the nearest drying kilns and selling agency, and before the days of the auger and bulk transport it had to be moved in sacks, even although you employed a tanker combine. Without drying plant and reserve storage space at home it was like the pearls before swine, because you were always at the mercy of down-grade prices in a glutted market, with no back door until prices stabilised. Moisture content and the quality of your cereal was another factor you couldn't argue much about once it was off your own premises, and you wouldn't want to cart it all home again. Another choice was propcorn saturation, a chemical which enabled you to store your barley ceiling high in your old corn loft or even in the empty byres; the snag was that your barley was no good for distillery malting or other human consumption and could only be used as cattle feed. But what of it? Our fathers sometimes preferred corn on the hoof to selling it in sacks at six shillings a bag, and the banker winked his approval.

Another machine which drove men from the farms was the robot turnip cutter. This machine, hitherto always believed to be impracticable, suddenly appeared on the scene with great success, moreso when a mechanical elevator was added to it, which made it possible to pluck and load turnips on to carts in one operation. This was in the early nineteen-sixties and it meant a colossal saving of labour on one of the most essential and sustained jobs in farming—turnip pulling—a drudgery that lasted from November to April, six months in the farming year and absorbing about 50 per cent of all manual effort in the fields. For the itinerant casual worker the laborious hand-pulling of turnips had always been a standby, and for general workers (orramen) and cattlemen it provided constant employment. For generations men had almost prostrated themselves in personal rivalry competing with each other in this back-breaking trial of endurance to be first to reach the end of a quarter mile drill, but now there was no honour in muscle power in the face of machinery. Henceforth general workers, unless they could drive a tractor were under threat of redundancy—a new word in the agricultural dictionary. But as with the horses it wasn't too soon, because experienced labour was getting scarce on the land; younger men had been leaving in droves for years and natural retirement was bringing a dearth of qualified labour, especially in the dairy byres.

The turnip-cutter revolutionised farming methods to at least the same extent as the combine-harvester; even moreso when it is remembered that this small machine (in comparison—besides being much cheaper) was no fair weather monstrosity that could only be used in a short season. It is also less vulnerable in foul weather because it can be used periodically when ground and sky are suitable, building up a store of turnips to last over the next downpour.

Turnip hoeing was another labour mainstay that has fallen victim to mechanisation, this time to the precision seed sower and relevant weed-killers, a method that has fallen far short of the manual hoe in cleaning a turnip field. While labour was still cheaper than machinery mechanisation was static, or at least intermittent with every wages spiral when redundancy increased and new machines were bought. Tractors became more sophisticated and implements more adaptable and wages had to be sacrificed to pay for them. Besides the combine-harvester and the turnip-cutter the catalogue includes the combine drill-sower (as compared to the broadcast machine); the manure spinner (a poor show compared with the old 'bone-davie'); disc harrows,

rotovator and ground-leveller, buckrake and muck-loader, and
of course the reversible plough, which is a real winner; the three-
drill plough and potato-harvester; and to handle the standing
crops we have the flail-mower, hay-turner, straw wuffler, baler
and sledge, straw elevators, round baler, fork lift, sprayer
plant—everything to save labour, and we even have computerised
milking and cow-feeding, the factory farm complete, and to think
that compressed oil in a rubber pipe can give muscle and movement to most of these machines is fantastic.

The domestic scene has also changed and the first to go was the
kitchiedeem, followed by the hens and the milk cows, the chaumer
chiels and the peat stack, the girnal and the milk churn, the spurtle
and the brose caup, the brookie pot and the scrubbing brush, the
washing tub and the clothes mangle—all are gone, including the
vanmen, and the family now live out of the refrigerator,
replenished by periodic visits in the car to the supermarket and the
pressure cooker and microwave have taken the place of the swey
over the oven range and the open fireplace, with its bellows, coal-
scuttle, tongs and poker; while house chores are lightened by
washing machine and spin-drier, dish-washer and carpet sweeper
so that the servant lassie wouldn't get a job nowadays.

To hold down my job towards the end of my farming life I had
to become a dogsbody. I had to learn to drive a tractor and
manipulate expensive machinery which increased my responsi-
bilities at a stage in life when I should have tried to minimise
them. In late middle-age I was doing jobs that didn't exist in my
youth, when I would have been more adaptable and mechanically minded; now I was an old dog having to learn new tricks,
taking advice from young grease-guns who weren't born when
I worked with their fathers. The change from physical effort to
joy-sticks was exasperating, my mind responding to clockwork
precision, my mental reflexes sharpened and nerve sprung,
tightening my grip on the steering wheel and directing my feet
on the unaccustomed pedals of industry. It was a trial case of
mind over matter, where a lifetime of experience meant nothing
in the chaotic change in my existence. My labours of nearly
half-a-century were obsolete. That I had been of the salt of the
earth became a disillusionment. Youth had overtaken my generation at the wheel of life. Yet ours had been a lifetime of
endurance and effort these young men would never be called

upon to tolerate. For over forty years I had justified my existence in agriculture on false pretences—on the grounds that we were indispensable to a consumer population. Even in wartime we had been rejected for military service. Continued employment was almost integral with our existence, a sort of natural built-in guarantee of perpetual service to the community. Alas it was a complacency that overtook us in the end. I never dreamed my generation would have to leave agriculture because it was becoming a specialised industry demanding skills beyond our capabilities. Unemployment contribution by farm workers became compulsory in 1936, but apart from a few individual and unfortunate cases we never required unemployment benefit. Now we had at last become victims of the machine which at first we had regarded as beneficent, but which now crushed us relentlessly and forced us aside.

Compared with the horsemen I was at a disadvantage, because when the horses were disposed of their drivers automatically went on the tractors that replaced them. Most of them acquired the necessary skills and settled down contentedly with the new environment, retiring as qualified tractormen. As a cattleman cum 'orraman' machinery had not interfered with my routine work to the same extent as it had done with the horsemen. Stockmen were roped in eventually when they had to get on a tractor to feed loose cattle in courts from the gangways and in the open fields, but by then I had left the byres and was employed on general duties, mostly assisting the tractormen on machines not then controlled from the tractors.

At age fifty-eight, in the rat race that was developing towards the final encroachment of machinery, I had to be more versatile in my duties than I had ever been in my youth. Besides the tractor work I had to relieve at week-ends in the dairy byres and work overtime on my tractor in the evenings, which made the day longer than it had ever been in the hardest days of the horse work. The staff had been reduced to less than half, from twelve to five, and those of us who remained had to make it up in man hours. My home life was narrowed to a margin and I had to stretch myself beyond my element. It was getting me down and for the first time in my life I earnestly wished to be out of the clamour which had overtaken a traditional consistency we had become accustomed to. The horse work was more laborious but there was a satisfaction in it and a sense of accomplishment and community spirit I could never associate with the new factory farming methods. There was a new cash register urgency in everying we did and it was a poor substitute for harmony in the fields. If the old system had prevailed for another decade I would have stayed on the land contentedly until I got my pension. But the machine age overtook me on the last lap and I was heart sick of the monster which now motivated and practically controlled our lives. He even came to bed with me and turned my pleasant dreams to nightmares. My working hours became a series of cliff-hangers, like sitting on a tractor hanging over the edge of a silage clamp with a twelve-foot drop, almost to certain death until I was chained back to sanity by an anxious tractormate who arrived just in time. What had been inherent routine now became a labyrinthian chase with danger at every bend. An occupation I had learned to endure and indeed almost to enjoy had now become unbearable for me. After a lifetime apprenticeship on the land it was humiliating that younger men had to instruct me in the use of equipment I had never handled and in some cases had never seen before.

But for all my short-comings don't imagine that I was by any means useless on a tractor. Far from it for I was quite efficient and managed to do everything expected of me. I had driven a car for ten years before then and I knew the basic mechanics of the thing. In fact I was catching up on the younger lads by the time I finished and could nip the tractor around with the best of them. But I was taxing my mental reflexes to accomplish it. I had never worried over muscle strain but having my mind taken over by a machine was something I resented. I am of a meditative composition and what had formerly been conducive to the comtemplative life was becoming a haywire entanglement beyond my endurance. I was getting in the way and the sooner I was out of the rat race the better—or so I thought, but as things turned out for me maybe I shouldn't have been so rash.

Leaving farm work was different from leaving a factory, because there was always a house to consider. Living in the city (or even in the country) so long as you had a fixed abode, you could change your job at any time, but not so as a cottar living in a tied house where work and home were one entity. You were like the snail with your house on your back, and crossing the road you could be crushed. Except for extreme cases of hardship, for which (thank goodness) I didn't qualify, the Regional Councils were not keen to accommodate families with a fit breadwinner from the land, and farmer members endorsed that policy. Even without a bathroom I had my name on the housing list for five years with no response. The farmer I was working for wouldn't give me tenancy of my cottage. He was putting a dairy cattleman into it, and because of the commotion in the labour market at the time I didn't blame him. My only alternative was to borrow money and buy a flat in the city, then look for a job. At my time in life that wasn't easy, and older men who had jobs were hanging on to them. I moved to Aberdeen in 1971 and applied for work with the Links and Parks Department. But there was a waiting list of 600 applicants and they wouldn't consider me even for an interview. My last resort was the marts at Kittybrewster, which never appealed to me but my back was to the wall and no dole for six weeks because I had left my last job voluntarily. For me the marts was the fag-end of the industry and my ideal of animal husbandry became a visionary bloodbath. Feeding and caring for animals was one thing, driving them to the slaughterhouse quite another; not that I ever had any mistaken illusions about the purpose of my former employment, but now that I was faced with the inevitable I abhorred it. After a severe nervous breakdown I found a situation with W Smith & Son, seedsmen and landscape gardeners at Hazlehead, where I was privileged to finish my working life in pleasant surroundings which made a gentle art of my former agricultural experience, and my four years of tractor work on the farms was very useful expertise on the larger contracts where tractors were employed.

Union membership was of no avail in these circumstances. Shop stewards are unheard of in agricultural redundancies. How could they close down a farm because the farmer had dismissed half of the staff? How could they stage a sit-in strike among food-starved animals or where milk was spouting from the inflamed udders of unmilked cows? Workers were entitled to redundancy payment in genuine cases but that didn't provide a house to live in. Some farmers allowed redundant workers to remain in their homes but not always. There were few unfair dismissals but when problems arose the Union bosses wouldn't handle anything that wasn't in writing, which it never was with farm servants. The relation between a farmer and his workers is so much more personal and intimate than it is between a factory hand and the general manager. The farmer can be your nearest neighbour and sometimes almost a personal friend and a nucleus of Union influence could never be formed in such a scattered community. The Union branches collected the monthly membership fees but beyond that they had no wish to become involved. They could have used their influence with the housing authorities in providing us with alternative accommodation independent of the farmers; but because of rents above our earning power, the former housing colonies intended for farm workers were occupied by commuters with city jobs so perhaps the unions didn't want to get their fingers burned. It was all so complicated until the occupant of a tied cottage was protected by law with an extension of tenancy to a period of six months after termination of employment, sometimes longer, but like most reforms it was a bit late in fitting safety locks after the burglary had been committed.

As a diary cattleman in my youth I was milking thirty-five cows with machines and considered to be doing a fairly good job. By the time I left the industry a man was capable of milking 100 cows single-handed, and had to be doing so to keep the industry viable. Of course he was being paid as much for a week's work as I earned in a whole year, and thereby the boomerang that has dislodged us.

And what of the end product—what are the results of mechanisation on the land? Have we benefited from modernisation or have we lost something of the flavour of the past? We would have to put these questions to a panel of experts as I am no longer involved in agricultural affairs. Speaking for myself I would say that we have lost nothing—apart from our jobs—and that the Sunday roast still tastes as good; even better for us because in the days I helped to produce the silverside or sirloin steak we couldn't afford to buy it. I was engaged in producing the finest of Scotch beef (in fact I once topped the show in carcass meat at Smithfield) but my wages could only afford my wife to buy meat to boil or stew, the cheaper cuts, mince and a bone to make soup, while the prime cuts went south to Sainsburys or some other of the London meat markets. Potatoes, turnips and vegetables are still as sweet though for us more expensive than growing our own.

Nowadays I pay 40p for a slice of turnip I used to get for the taking. Milk is still plentiful and healthy and cheaper than soft drinks. Oatmeal is just as good in the porridge and the bacon and egg has not suffered all that much from being factory produced.

On the surface then it would appear that agriculture is still in a healthy state. When I go to the country and look across the fields they are just as pleasant and fruitful as ever they were, especially in the late spring when the grass is richly green. There are still straight drills and furrows to rest the eye on and to prove that men do still take a pride in their work. Most arable fields are still cultivated and the cattle and sheep browse contentedly on the sunny braes. Perhaps the absence of horses and corn stacks and the empty cottages is the only real evidence of change. The ruined deserted crofts are also part of the story, and the farm chaumers where the lum never reeks nowadays. I have one sad complaint and that is the untidiness of the farmtoons nowadays. Implements and machinery are lying about everywhere and at most of the steadings a stranger would think they were all preparing for a roup, only the articles for sale are too haphazard even for that. What has happened to all the big sheds that were built on grant aid on the plea that they were to hold machinery against damp and deterioration? Are the great barns stacked with baled straw or hay or just standing empty? By late summer some of the implements are out of sight in long waving grass and thistles and tanzies (ragwort) abound in the farmyards. Surely these farmers have forgotten what the old grieves used to say when they armed us with scythes and sent us thistle cutting around the fields

> Cut in June, cut too soon,
> Cut in July, cut to die!

There are some tidy farms with not a docken or burry (Scotch) thistle to be seen about the doors and the close tarred or concreted and all the ploughshares under a roof. But these tidy farms are in the minority and are probably the ones who kept the orraman on the wage bill, for he was the one who used to keep the steadings tidy, who swept the farm close or scraped up the dubs, cut the thistles, repaired the fences and built up the dykes. He was the first to be got rid of and the farmtoons have never looked the same since. I know he never added a penny to the bank deposit (except when he was with the other lads) but he tidied the back shop and arranged the window display. He was good advertising and in our age of pressurized salesmanship surely he would be worth his salt lick. Perhaps he would tidy up the mess created by the rat race in agriculture. It would be a small price to pay for his services.

In the foregoing documentary I haven't mentioned the shepherds, though they were regarded as key men with the grieves and head cattlemen and respected or despised according to temperament. But the sheepfold was one department in agriculture that couldn't be mechanised, and apart from improved methods in shearing and dipping has remained almost as it was in Biblical times, from the days of Jacob and his lambs. 'One Man and His Dog' on TV is enough to convince us that there are still shepherds on the farms.

PLEASURABLY REMINDED

Review of *The Cornkister Days* by
David Kerr Cameron (Gollancz, London)
By courtesy of *The Leopard*, Aberdeen

They are gone from the plough, those men I once knew—and from the harrow and the hyow and the sounds of harvest. Their days are already receding, a part of our folk culture; their world has faded before the march of agri-business and agri-technology. All are figures in a far landscape and maybe the land is poorer now: who can say, one way or the other? . . . They were all of them men of the land and with them has gone much of the countryside's old culture, most of the rituals that linked us with the farming past— the countryside they yearly recreated. . . . War was the watershed, the thing that divided us from our rural yesterdays. Farming marched on increasingly into the province of the engineer and scientist. . . . The machine-age farming would erode that old affinity of men with the soil and the seasons, or at least sadly diminish it. It would rob the landscape of much of its ancient architecture, the patterns of the hayfield and harvest, and all the rhythms of the horse-drawn age.

So writes David Kerr Cameron in the last chapter of his book *The Cornkister Days*, the last in his trilogy on the old lowland farmtouns.

For a man who never worked on the old farmtouns, except perhaps for a wee while before he entered journalism, it is such a thoroughly comprehensive record that with all my experience on the land I couldn't improve on it. The journalistic scope and research of his subject is so very wide and accurate there is little I could add to it or correct and certainly nothing I could hold up to ridicule. However, seeing that I am one of the old bogie-smoking 'barra-bailies' he so fondly laments I will elucidate on one or two points if only to show how little rope Mr Cameron has left for me to 'kinch up' after he has wound his 'cloo' (ball).

The grubber for instance was never to my knowledge used on cereal crops, only on root tillage, turnips and sometimes potatoes if the spring-harrow was insufficient in raising a tilth. The grubber on lea tore up too many sods and the torry worm larva that surfaced with the turf and would soon deplete a corn brier. The heavy disc harrow that replaced the grubber in the tractor age made lea turnips practicable without surfacing the sods and the results were better (even without dung) than turnips on stubble that were poorer in nitrogen after a corn crop.

As an old stockman myself I was particularly interested in the chapter on Byres and Bailies, and one of the things that Mr Cameron omitted was the fact that cattle chains sometimes grew into their necks if neglected as the animals got fatter, and that these shackles were each fitted with a swivel to prevent choking or strangulation in the stalls. Compared with the pig and the hen the machine age has been kind to the oxen; the neck chains of their claustrophobic past have been discarded and they *all* now enjoy the freedom of open courts. The barra-bailies never weighed their cattle feed and they scorned at college folk who said they should. They knew instinctively what was enough for a beast, and by watching the laxative consistency of their dung they varied the quantity accordingly, especially with turnips which provided the moisture content of the diet. Cattle with dry coats and hard dung never did well on the weighbridge and lack of turnips in an unbalanced menu was the cause of it. The old bailies were wizards at their jobs and the farmers knew it. Sliced turnips is another omission, and the 'plump-hasher' that crumpled and aged mony a cattle bailie long before his time. 'It was aye the time that gaed deen in the byre—niver the wark!'

About the only thing left out for me to carp about is the detail of how easy it was to insert cart-wheel pins upside-down when you was greasing the axle with your horse between the shafts and your cart backed on to its stoups so that you could spin the wheels. Of course the wheel came off on the road and this was a disaster when you were loaded with ten sacks of oats for the granary. See the chapter on 'The Gold of Autumn'. Sharps or steel diamonds were also hammered into the slots in the horse-shoes so that they could keep their feet on ice and sliddery roads, but Mr Cameron may have touched on some of these details in his other books.

In the chapter on 'Old Alignments' I would add that the bigger touns didn't always fill their barns with corn sheaves before threshing. Some of them held only one load at the drum-bench and the sheaves were carted in by two carts alternately while threshing was in progress, one loading in the stackyard and the other driver forking his sheaves to the man feeding the barn mill.

To swing a newly built cornstack (or even in mid-winter) it wasn't necessary to plunge the hands, armpit deep, into the ruck and grab hold of two sheaves to accomplish it. I could swing my stacks the said six-inches with a fingertip hold on two-inch of stubble-end at shoulder level. That was what the grieve liked to see. I too have worn knee patches on my dungarees (sewn on by my wife for the season) and I have crawled round and round on the rucks for a fortnight till my knees were numb. I have snatched a sheaf-a-second from the forker with my right hand until my fingerprints were worn off and my fingertips were so tender I could scarcely tie my pints in the morning or hold a spoon at mealtimes; especially if there were thistles in the crop, mostly concealed in the heart of a sheaf and you couldn't avoid them.

And I too have taken a dander roon the cornyard smokin' ma pipe in the licht o' the hairst meen, nae tae admire ma wark but tae see if ma rucks were still on the plumb, and if they werena I'd put a prop in faur they needed it tae strauchen them up afore they sat doon. It was a case o' the stitch in time here and wis better deen fin yer ruck wis new biggit. These 'ruck-posts' were bought from the forresters or the saw-mill still with the bark on and a good grieve liked a builder whose stacks occasionally required them. It was a sign that his rucks were 'weel he'rtet' and would run watter like aff a deuk's back. Farmers kept their old cart-shafts for ruck-posts and old ladders were also useful.

Nowadays we don't have cornstacks, but giant tissue rolls of compressed straw in the stubble fields. In mid-summer our farming landscape is a Dutch patchwork in the Daffodil gold of the rape-seed flower, soon to be matched I am told by the speedwell blue of flax blossom. The farming year has gone haywire and seedtime and harvest are simultaneous, combine and plough at cross purposes in a crazy juxtaposition of the seasons, a harnessing of nature by technology and science in a landscape of black and gold.

Mr Cameron quotes freely from the Bothy Ballads, but 'Aul Johnny Bruce o' the Corner' was 'Aul Johnny Bruce o' the Fornet' as I remember him. Be that as it may, the ballads had changed their tune by the time I was in my prime, maybe with a touch of glamour and sophistication that had never been known to the older chaumer chiels. Let me quote the following, which appeared in the *People's Journal* for 15 March 1947.

> Back to the land! Hark to the clarion call,
> As sounded, huskily, by Miss Bacall;
> Shall idle, untilled acres plead in vain?
> Not while there's still a Rustle left in Jane.
>
> The charms of Rita Hayworth will inspire
> The man morosely mucking out the byre.
> 'For ploy—for Loy!' rings out the solemn vow,
> The Grable legs will help to speed the plough.
>
> As o'er the fertile land the grey dawn breaks,
> The soundly slumb'ring labourer awakes;
> Upon his lips the cry, 'Toujours, Lamarr!'
> He's off to hitch his waggon to a Star.

etc., with acknowledgement to J C H G, a budding poet of the nineteen forties.

Mr Cameron has done an excellent job and it is a book that had to be written before the memory fades. There is much in his book that I admire; much that I had forgotten, but of which I am here pleasurably reminded. With his early farming background and journalistic experience—and above all, by his abiding interest in agriculture, we are indebted for his enthusiasm in preserving a breath of our swiftly vanishing culture and folklore.